# Models for Multidisciplinary Arrangements

*A State-by-State Review of Options*

# APA PRACTITIONER'S TOOLBOX SERIES

# Models for Multidisciplinary Arrangements

## A State-by-State Review of Options

American Psychological Association Practice Directorate
with
McDermott, Will, & Emery

AMERICAN PSYCHOLOGICAL ASSOCIATION
Washington, DC

A *Cautionary Note:*

This manual was written to serve both as a reference and as a tool to help providers practice more efficiently in a changing, demanding marketplace. The information contained herein is accurate and complete to the best of our knowledge. However, *Models for Multidisciplinary Arrangements: A State-by State Review of Options* should be read with the understanding that it is meant as a supplement, not a substitute, for sound legal, accounting, business, or other professional consulting services. When such services are required, the assistance of a competent professional should be sought.

Published by
American Psychological Association
750 First Street, NE
Washington, DC 20002

Copies may be ordered from
APA Order Department
P.O. Box 2710
Hyattsville, MD 20784

Composition and Printing: National Academy Press, Washington, DC
Cover Designer: Leigh Coriale

**ISBN: 1-55798-363-1**


**British Library Cataloguing-In-Publication Data**
A CIP record is available from the British Library

*Printed in the United States of America*
*First Edition*

# Contents

AMERICAN
PSYCHOLOGICAL
ASSOCIATION

Dear Colleague:

The American Psychological Association Practice Directorate is pleased to offer <u>Models for</u>
<u>Multidisciplinary Arrangements: A State-By-State Review of Options</u> as one component of the
"APA Practitioner's Toolbox Series."  This series of books is designed to help the practicing
psychologist build a successful practice in an environment which requires attention to an
increasingly complex approach to healthcare while maintaining the quality of services for which
psychology has become known.  This particular book, written in conjunction with the Washington,
D.C. law firm of McDermott, Will & Emery, is intended to outline the options available for
psychologists interested in multidisciplinary practice arrangements.

A growing trend in the changing healthcare system is for healthcare professionals from various
disciplines to team up in some form of joint practice to provide a more diverse array of services
than is possible under solo practice arrangements.   While group practices comprised of
psychologists are able to provide a wide variety of services (e.g., pediatric, child, adolescent, adult,
clinical neuropsychology, rehabilitative, forensic services), even greater diversity is possible when
psychologists join together with other professionals.  The resulting multidisciplinary arrangements
may include primary care physicians, psychiatrists, psychologists, and other mental health
professionals such as social workers, marriage/family therapists, and professional counselors.
However, some states' laws restrict the ways in which psychologists can affiliate with non-
psychologists to provide healthcare services.

<u>Models for Multidisciplinary Arrangements: A State-by State Review of Options</u> describes and
analyzes several types of alliances through which psychologists may optimize their association with
other providers.   The book not only addresses the advantages and disadvantages of various
multidisciplinary arrangements, but it also reviews feasible options on a state-by-state basis in light
of specific state laws and the legal ramifications of choosing a particular arrangement.  While the
book is clearly not intended to replace appropriate legal consultation for those psychologists wishing
to pursue multidisciplinary practice, it provides a framework for psychologists to consider which
type of arrangement is likely to be most beneficial.  The book thereby facilitates practitioners'
choosing an effective structure for their practices that will enhance professional opportunities to
provide quality psychological services to health care consumers.

Sincerely,

Russ Newman, Ph.D., J.D.
Executive Director for Professional Practice

750 First Street, NE
Washington, DC 20002-4242
(202) 336-5913
(202) 336-5797 Fax
(202) 336-6123 TDD

Russ Newman, Ph.D., J.D.
*Executive Director*
*Practice Directorate*

# Preface

As a result of the expansion in insurance coverage for mental health care services, a substantial percentage of Americans have third-party insurance for professional psychological services. Increasingly, however, this development is creating significant problems for psychologists as more payers are limiting patients' ability to choose their own therapists as well as the number of treatment sessions that will be covered. In many cases, patients are given strong incentives to choose psychologists or other health care professionals who are members of the payer's network of preferred providers. These incentives typically take the form of patient coinsurance obligations that are significantly lower for the services of network providers than for nonnetwork providers. Indeed, it is not uncommon for patients to have no coverage at all for services by nonnetwork providers.

Additional pressure is placed on mental health care providers owing to the growing role of mental health management firms, such as Merit, Green Spring, Value Behavioral Health, and United Behavioral Health. These firms typically enter into "carve-out" arrangements either directly with self-insured employers or as subcontractors to health maintenance organizations or other insurers. Under such an arrangement, a mental health management firm assumes financial and/or administrative responsibility for the mental health services required by persons covered by a particular plan. As part of its cost containment strategy, the mental health management firm typically establishes small preferred provider networks and offers beneficiaries strong incentives to select a network therapist.

In this environment many psychologists are considering working in some way with other psychologists and physicians (particularly psychiatrists and/or primary care physicians), and possibly with other mental health professionals as well, for several reasons. First, some payers (or mental health management firms), in assembling their provider networks, may be more interested in contracting with a relatively small number of provider groups as opposed to signing individual contracts with a large number of solo practitioners. Becoming part of such a group thus increases the ability of an individual psychologist to become a member of such networks.

Second, in many parts of the country, primary care physicians (family practitioners, general practitioners, internists, pediatricians) are increasingly being asked (and in some cases are actively seeking) to assume more of the financial risk for the total cost of health care services, including mental health services. As primary care physicians take on this financial responsibility, they tend to make fewer referrals for mental health services. Mental health professionals who are closely aligned with such physicians are likely to have more referrals from their patients.

Finally, a large alliance of practitioners may ultimately be in a position to compete directly with mental health management firms, by entering into carve-out arrangements directly with employers or other payers. Obviously, such an alliance needs to be competitive economically with existing firms if it expects to capture contracts. Furthermore, even if such an alliance is able to secure contracts, it will need substantial information and management resources to administer those contracts. Nonetheless, it may be possible for an alliance of professionals that is owned and controlled by the providers themselves to deliver cost-effective care, free of the intrusive utilization controls imposed by management firms.

## OVERVIEW

This book describes and analyzes several types of alliances through which psychologists join together with physicians (including psychiatrists and primary care physicians) and/or other mental health care professionals (such as social workers, marriage/family therapists, and professional counselors). The types of alliances discussed here can be divided into two categories. The distinction between the two categories is primarily based on how bills are issued for services rendered by the members of the alliance. The first category consists of arrangements in which a single entity bills for the services of its member practitioners. The second category consists of arrangements in which practitioners are linked together through a series of contracts but bill separately for their own services. Arrangements that fall into the first category typically, but not always, involve substantially more integration than the second model.

# Acknowledgments

We are grateful for the contributions of the following people, whose hard work and assistance made this book possible: the McDermott, Will and Emery staff, headed by Wendy L. Krasner (J.D.) and Bryan Puterbaugh; Russ Newman (Ph.D., J.D.); C. Henry Engleka; Shirley Higuchi (J.D); Cherie Jones (J.D); Neela Agarwalla (J.D); and the Practice Directorate Marketing staff, including Chris Vein, Craig Olswang, and Garth Huston.

# 1

# General Discussion of Arrangements

**P**RACTITIONERS WHO *wish to integrate their practices have a number of options, depending on state law. This chapter discusses options in which the integrated entity bills for practitioners' services in the name of the entity, using a provider number assigned to it. The focus here is on three types of legal entities: partnerships, corporations, and limited liability companies.*

## INTEGRATED MODELS

It is important to realize that the choice of a legal structure does not resolve the numerous operational and governance issues that arise in connection with the formation of an integrated group. Practitioners who want to integrate their practices must agree in advance on who will make the operational decisions and how. These decisions can range from the relatively mundane (e.g., what the name of the group will be) to ones with potentially significant consequences (e.g., how profits will be allocated, whether to bring other practitioners into the group, whether to enter into a particular managed care contract). All of the practitioners might retain an equal voice in virtually every management decision or they can delegate most decisions to a manager or a management committee, reserving key decisions for a vote of all the practitioners. Within the constraints imposed by state law, each of the legal vehicles addressed here is flexible enough to accommodate the choices and preferences of group members regarding these organizational and operational issues.

It is also important to recognize that the entity that bills for the practitioners' services need not own all of the assets used by the practice. It is common for a separate entity (which can be owned by all, or only some, of the same practitioners) to hold title to the group's office space and equipment; such an entity is often termed a management services organization (MSO). Similarly, when a single group is formed by combining several formerly independent practices, it is not uncommon for group members to remain in their own offices rather than move to a shared space. In such arrangements, called "group practices without walls," individual practitioners often continue to own the assets of their former practices; they then rent those assets to the combined group based on some mutually acceptable formula. Whether one of these variations is desirable for any given group depends primarily on the tax and financial situations of the participating practitioners.

### Partnerships

A multidisciplinary partnership can be formed, unless prohibited by state law, by partners who include any combination of psychologists, psychiatrists, primary care physicians, and others. Such a partnership can bill for the services of the practitioners who are its partners and any others who are employees of the partnership.

Operating as a partnership has tax advantages over operating as a corporation, because only the partners, not the partnership itself, are taxed. That is, if the partnership has been properly structured, it does not pay taxes directly; rather, each partner is taxed on his or her share of the partnership's net income or losses. In contrast, a corporation itself is taxed when it makes a profit and then its shareholders are also taxed when they receive dividends from the corporation. (As discussed later, the problem of double taxation of corporations can often be reduced through the use of "S corporations.")

When deciding on a legal structure for an integrated group, an important consideration is the extent to which group members may be held personally liable for the negligence of other practitioners in the group.[1] A psychologist who is a partner in a general partnership can be held personally liable (i.e., the personal assets of the partner, not just the money invested by the partner in the partnership, are at risk) for all obligations of the partnership. These may include damages caused by actions of other partners, damages caused by actions of employees of the partnership, and business debts of the partnership (e.g., rent payments under a partnership's lease).[2] Of course, a partnership can purchase malpractice insurance. However, the partners will be personally liable for any amount not covered by insurance. Potentially unlimited personal liability makes a general partnership much less attractive than a corporation for health care practitioners.

In some states practitioners can organize as a limited liability partnership (LLP). This structure is a relatively recent innovation. The distinction between an LLP and a general partnership is that, if one partner in an LLP negligently injures a patient, the patient is entitled to be compensated only from the assets of the LLP itself and the personal assets of the partner who treated the patient. The patient may not force the other partners to contribute their personal assets. The partners of an LLP, however, typically remain personally liable for the LLP's business debts (e.g., rent payments).

While a general partnership may operate without filing any special application with the state in which it operates, an LLP must file the appropriate application forms and be registered. Periodic filings may be required to maintain the liability protection of the LLP structure.

It is important to distinguish LLPs from two types of entities having similar names: limited liability companies (LLCs) and limited partnerships. LLCs are discussed in chapter 3. A limited partnership is a special type of partnership in which a small number of general partners accept complete personal liability for the debts of the partnership, while the other investors (known as limited partners) are insulated from personal liability. By law, limited partners are not permitted to play an active role in the management of the limited partnership. Limited partnerships are generally not a suitable structure for professional practices because practitioners who have an ownership interest in the practice usually want to have an active voice in its management. Moreover, few practitioners are willing to assume responsibility as general partners for the malpractice liability of all the limited partners.

### Corporations

Corporations have several features that distinguish them from partnerships. An owner of a corporation is liable for the debts of the corporation, regardless of how they arise, only up to the amount of his or her investment in the corporation.

Corporations typically centralize their management in a board of directors and elected officers. Only the officers of the corporation, acting under authority granted by the board, may sign contracts for the corporation. A corporation continues to exist even when one or more shareholders sell their shares.

As noted earlier, a corporation's profits are usually taxed twice: once when the corporation earns them and a second time when it distributes them to its shareholders in the form of dividends. However, corporations often escape federal income taxes by electing to be treated as an "S corporation." An S corporation must have no more than 35 shareholders, all of whom are individuals, and only one class of voting stock. S corporations are taxed like partnerships; that is, the net income and losses of the corporation are "passed through" for tax purposes to the corporation's shareholders, who pay taxes individually on their share of the corporation's earnings or losses. Depending on state law, S corporations may also be exempt from state income taxes. Moreover, even if a professional service entity does not qualify as an S corporation, it can often "zero out" its books—and thereby avoid taxation—by distributing excess earnings to shareholders in the form of year-end bonuses.

Relatively few states permit ordinary corporations (commonly termed "business corporations") to employ physicians and psychologists and to bill in the name of the corporation for their professional services. In states that do permit business corporations to engage in such activities, such entities provide a straightforward vehicle for assembling a multidisciplinary practice.

A few states (e.g., Michigan) that prohibit for-profit business corporations from hiring psychologists, physicians, and other health care professionals nonetheless permit nonprofit corporations (sometimes known as "nonstock corporations") to do so. A nonprofit corporation may not pay dividends to its members, but it may pay reasonable salaries to its employees, even when those employees are also members or officers of the corporation. A nonprofit corporation can thus be a viable vehicle for professional practices, despite the "nonprofit" label.

A nonprofit corporation is managed by officers under the direction of a board of directors. The persons with ultimate control over the activities of a nonprofit corporation are typically known as members of the corporation, rather than shareholders.

The fact that a corporation is denominated nonprofit does not mean that it is exempt from income taxes. Such corporations will be taxed if they earn a profit, unless they meet stringent requirements for tax exemption (e.g., provision of charity care and limited control by practitioners); few if any entities that are dominated by health care practitioners will be able to qualify for tax exemption.

In many states the "corporate practice of medicine" doctrine bars both for-profit business corporations and nonprofit corporations from employing, and billing for the services of, psychologists and physicians. In these states the only type of corporation that may engage in these practices is a "professional corporation" (or PC).

The PC laws of each state govern the ownership, management, and operation of these corporations.[3] As indicated by the state-by-state analysis in chapter 3, the laws vary substantially among the states. For example, some states explicitly allow, while other states explicitly forbid, PCs to have shareholders who are licensed in different professions. In states that require all of a PC's shareholders to be licensed in the same profession, a PC that has physician shareholders cannot have shareholders who are psychologists. Some states require that a PC's officers, directors, and professional employees hold the same type of license as the PC's shareholders; other states do not. Where a psychologist may be a director or officer of a physician-owned PC, the psychologist may be able to influence the operations of the PC by voting as a director or acting as an officer even if he or she cannot have a direct ownership interest in the corporation.

The PC framework allows, but does not require, tight integration of practices. Typically, each practitioner signs a full-time employment agreement with the PC. The practitioner's compensation may be a fixed salary or may include bonus payments for productivity.

### Limited Liability Companies (LLCs)

Statutes authorizing LLCs have been enacted in nearly all 50 states in the past several years. LLCs are hybrids with some of the best characteristics of both corporations and partnerships. LLCs have "members," who are analogous to the shareholders of a corporation or the partners of a partnership. Members of an LLC have limited liability for the liabilities of the LLC, including both ordinary business obligations and liabilities arising out of the professional malpractice of other members or employees of the LLC. At the same time, a properly structured LLC is taxed as a partnership under federal law and the laws of most states (but not Florida or Texas).

An LLC is typically formed by filing articles of organization with the appropriate state authorities. An LLC must have an "operating agreement," which essentially serves as its constitution. The operating agreement specifies how the LLC will be governed, how profits and losses will be allocated, and similar issues. All members can take an active role in the LLC's management, or the LLC can centralize its management in managers, who function like the officers of a corporation.

In some states it is clear that an LLC may employ psychologists, physicians, and other professionals and that it can bill in its own name for the services of those practitioners.[4]   In other states the authority of LLCs to engage in such activities remains unsettled.  Where it is clear that an LLC may engage in these activities, organization as an LLC may be the best vehicle for multidisciplinary health care practices.

## CONTRACTUAL AFFILIATIONS

It is not necessary for providers to actually integrate their practices into a single legal entity in order to be able to contract jointly with third-party payers.  Rather, it is possible for psychologists, physicians, and other practitioners to form an entity that serves as a contracting vehicle but that allows them to retain their separate practices.  Contracting vehicles of this type are known by a number of different names; here the term "network" will be used.[5]

Networks do not employ practitioners; instead, they enter into contracts with them.  Practitioners may practice as individuals or be organized as partnerships, corporations, or LLCs.  These agreements typically obligate the network to negotiate with third-party payers on behalf of the practitioners.  Once a network signs a contract with a payer, the network notifies all of the practitioners with whom it has agreements of the payment terms agreed to by the payer and any unique requirements (e.g., referral procedures).

Depending on state law, networks may enter into a number of different financial arrangements with payers.  In most states, networks may contract on a capitated basis (i.e., a network accepts a fixed amount of money per month for each person covered by the network regardless of the actual quantity or type of services that the member requires); however, as discussed below, capitation often triggers additional regulatory requirements.  When a network enters into a capitation arrangement, it is up to the network to determine how to allocate the capitated payments among its members.  More commonly, a network will negotiate a fee-for-service arrangement in which its members are paid, at rates specified by the payer, for each individual service they provide.  In such cases, practitioners generally bill the payer directly, although the network may handle billing and collection functions as the agent of the individual practitioners.  The ongoing expenses of operating the network can be funded by charging an administrative fee to the members, a network access fee to payers, or both.

A network typically negotiates with only some of the payers in a community. Practitioners who are members of the network are typically free to sign contracts with other payers outside the network, although it may be possible to design a network that restricts a member's ability to enter into contracts independently of the network or that requires members to give the best (i.e., lowest) price to the network.

It is usually best to organize a practitioner-sponsored network as a nonprofit corporation. The founding practitioners become the members of the network, contribute its start-up capital, and are empowered to vote on key decisions and elect the network's officers. A network can be established with multiple classes of members, and its bylaws may require all classes of members to consent to certain decisions, in order to protect the interests of each group. For example, psychologists could make up one class of members and physicians another. While networks can be established as for-profit corporations, state and federal laws regarding the issuance of securities may make the process more expensive and burdensome. Moreover, networks generally are structured to return any available funds in the form of provider payments rather than dividends.

Despite its status as a nonprofit corporation, a network formed for the purpose of contracting with third-party payers will almost certainly not be able to meet the standards for exemption from income taxes. Thus, to the extent a network has taxable income, it will be subject to federal and state income taxes.

Networks are usually not licensed or directly regulated by states. In New York, however, networks are subject to very substantial restrictions. There a network that wants to contract with health maintenance organizations (HMOs) must be licensed as an IPA, and each IPA may contract with only a single HMO. Moreover, two recent opinions by the New York Department of Health indicate that networks may not contract directly with any type of payer other than an HMO.

The liability of a network for claims arising from services provided by its members is uncertain. In the current environment, no entity is ever entirely insulated from lawsuits. However, to the extent a network acts solely as a contracting vehicle and does not attempt to review either the professional qualifications of its members or the quality or quantity of the services they render, the network's exposure should be limited. On the other hand, the more involved the network becomes in provider credentialing, utilization review, quality assurance, and similar activities, the greater the risks it will face and the more important it is for the network to secure appropriate insurance coverage.

The network model of provider contracting has advantages for psychologists.  A psychologist who is a member of a network is less likely to encounter interference with his or her professional autonomy than one who is part of a more tightly integrated group practice.  Also important is the fact that, if a psychologist decides such an arrangement is not beneficial, it is usually easier to leave a network than an integrated group.  Termination of a practitioner's contract with a network is usually effective within 30 to 90 days of giving notice, although a psychologist may be bound for a longer period by the payer agreements negotiated by the network that he or she accepted earlier.

Organization as a network has drawbacks though, too.  The flexibility afforded by the network structure also makes it harder to ensure that the entity will operate in a coordinated way.  The fact that a network member who is dissatisfied can leave the network with relative ease means that decisions must effectively be made by consensus, which can prevent the group from making difficult choices.  Moreover, and of greater significance, third-party payers may not be interested in contracting with networks, preferring instead to deal with more tightly integrated groups.

Antitrust laws present a particularly important constraint for network-type organizations.  While a full-scale discussion of antitrust laws is beyond the scope of this book, the basic concept is that they prohibit competitors from making collective decisions regarding with whom they will deal and what they will charge for their services.  With respect to antitrust laws, persons or entities are considered competitors if they are engaged in the same general line of business in a single geographical area.

As a rule, members of a truly integrated group are permitted to make collective contracting decisions because in the eyes of the law they are coventurers, not competitors.  Similarly, when a network enters into a capitation arrangement, its members will likely be viewed as coventurers (and not competitors) to the extent they share the risk that the cost of services required by patients will exceed what was anticipated.

However, when competing practitioners form a network-type organization and that network enters into fee-for-service arrangements, the law continues to view the network members as competitors.  Accordingly, the network must be structured such that each member is given the opportunity to make an *independent* decision about the rates he or she will accept.  Typically, this is accomplished by having the network develop a base fee schedule and presenting that model fee schedule to each network member for his or her consideration.  A network member who accepts the base schedule agrees to participate in all payer contracts where the payment rates are at least as high as the rates contained in the base schedule. This process allows the network to promise payers who accept the base fee schedule a guaranteed level of participation from network members.[6]

A second key issue that networks must take into account involves state insurance regulations. Some states take the position that, when a network accepts capitation or enters into another arrangement in which it assumes substantial financial risk, the network is engaging in the business of insurance and must obtain a state insurance license. Virtually all states permit networks to accept capitation from HMOs, and some states permit networks to accept capitation from licensed insurers as well. However, it is rare for a state to permit a network to enter into a capitation arrangement directly with a self-insured employer. A full exploration of state-level insurance issues is beyond the scope of this book, but practitioners interested in forming a network that will assume risk to any degree must first give careful consideration to those issues.

## EMPLOYMENT ARRANGEMENTS

The focus of this book is on ways by which psychologists can organize, and have a controlling interest in, alliances with other practitioners. It is important to note that such alliances can often be accomplished more simply and directly through an arrangement in which a psychologist acts as an *employee* of a physician or physician group. Obviously, such an arrangement may afford the psychologist less control than one in which he or she is also an owner of the practice. However, it is frequently possible to negotiate a long-term employment contract that provides a substantial degree of job security. Such a contract can include provisions that are responsive to the psychologist's concerns with respect to professional autonomy, working conditions, and so forth. Further, as noted above, in some state, laws governing PCs permit nonshareholders to act as corporate officers or directors. In those states an agreement might be negotiated that guarantees the psychologist a seat on the employer's board of directors even though he or she may not be a shareholder in the practice.

# 2

# Individual State Summary and Recommendations

I IN ALL 50 STATES, *psychologists, physicians, and other profes-*
*sionals may form a network for the purpose of joint contracting*
*with third-party payers.*[7] *With respect to more tightly integrated affili-*
*ations, what is feasible in individual states varies widely. The models*
*that are most likely to be attractive in each state are identified below. In*
*a number of states other models also are possible and might be prefer-*
*able in certain circumstances. Because of liability concerns, general*
*partnerships are not favored unless all other options are foreclosed by*
*state law.*

## ALABAMA

The business corporation appears to be the best option for multi-disciplinary practices in Alabama. Joint partnerships also are permissible.

## ALASKA

The limited liability company (LLC) is the most attractive option for multidisciplinary professional practices in Alaska. Professional corporations (PCs) and business corporations also may be viable, but these are less certain.

## ARIZONA

The most advantageous organizational form for multidisciplinary arrangements in Arizona appears to be the Professional LLC (PLLC).

## ARKANSAS

The LLC, which allows joint membership and employment of physicians and psychologists, appears to be the best option for practitioner integration in Arkansas.

## CALIFORNIA

The PC is the most attractive model for integration of psychologists and physicians in California. Although a PC must be formed "primarily" for the practice of a single profession (e.g., medicine *or* psychology), psychologists may be minority shareholders, as well as officers and directors, of medical PCs. Conversely, physicians may be minority shareholders, as well as officers and directors, of a PC that is formed primarily for the rendering of psychological services.

## COLORADO

In Colorado a general partnership is the only organizational form in which physicians and psychologists may practice jointly. It is unclear at present whether comembership in the more desirable LLC form is permissible.

## CONNECTICUT

Connecticut law permits the inclusion of physicians and psychologists as partners in a general partnership and in an LLP. Because the corporate practice of medicine doctrine has not been enforced in Connecticut, it may also be possible to offer multidisciplinary services through a business corporation.

## DELAWARE

LLCs are allowed to provide the professional services of both physicians and psychologists and are the most attractive option for practitioner integration in Delaware. Employment by a business corporation also is an option, as are multidisciplinary general partnerships and LLPs.

## DISTRICT OF COLUMBIA

The LLP and PLLC entities are the best choices for a joint mental health practice in the District of Columbia. Although the law is less clear as to other corporate forms, it is likely that business corporations and PCs also may conduct such a practice.

## FLORIDA

With the abolition of restrictions against the corporate practice of the learned professions in Florida, the best options for integrating psychology and medical practices appear to be business corporations and LLCs.

## GEORGIA

The LLC appears to be the preferred vehicle for integrating medicine and psychology practices in Georgia.

## HAWAII

The PC appears to be the best organizational structure for multi-disciplinary practices in Hawaii. Joint partnerships also are permissible.

## IDAHO

The Idaho PC and PLLC laws appear to allow joint psychologist/physician practices, making either an attractive option. Joint partnerships and LLPs are viable options.

## ILLINOIS

The most advantageous form for joint practice in Illinois is a physician-owned LLC with psychologist employees. The only other option is for a physician partnership to employ psychologists.

## INDIANA

Indiana LLCs are permitted to provide the professional services of both physicians and psychologists, and therefore constitute the best organizational option in Indiana. PCs and LLPs are options.

## IOWA

Although Iowa law is not definitive, it appears that LLPs, business corporations, PCs, and LLCs are all permissible forms of organization for physicians and psychologists to conduct a joint practice.

## KANSAS

Provided the incorporators are duly licensed, the PC and LLC appear to be the best structural options for multidisciplinary practices in Kansas. Joint partnerships and LLPs are permissible.

## KENTUCKY

The most advantageous options for multidisciplinary practices in Kentucky are the business corporation and the LLC.

## LOUISIANA

LLPs and business corporations are options for multidisciplinary practices in Louisiana. LLCs may probably also be formed for this purpose.

## MAINE

It appears that general partnerships are the only viable form of organization for multidisciplinary practices in Maine at this time.

## MARYLAND

The LLC form allows physicians and psychologists to practice together as members or employees and is thus the most advantageous organizational form in Maryland. Joint partnerships and LLPs are options; the relevant licensing boards have not made clear whether a physician/psychologist PC would be permitted.

## MASSACHUSETTS

Massachusetts PCs may render both physician and psychologist services; therefore, the PC appears to be the preferred form of organization.

## MICHIGAN

At this time, only two models appear to be viable in Michigan for integrating psychologists' and physicians' practices: a taxable nonprofit corporation and a general partnership.

## MINNESOTA

The only model that appears to be viable in Minnesota at this time is the general partnership.

## MISSISSIPPI

Mississippi physicians and psychologists may avail themselves of the business corporation, PC, or LLC forms of organization.

## MISSOURI

LLPs, PCs, and LLCs all appear to represent viable options for joint mental health practices under Missouri law.

## MONTANA

As long as certain medical practice rules are observed, the LLP, PC, and LLC entities are all available to physicians and psychologists who want to practice together in Montana.

## NEBRASKA

Although there is some uncertainty regarding Nebraska law, it appears that mental health professionals may form joint PCs and LLCs.

## NEVADA

While Nevada law is unclear about permissible entities for multidisciplinary professional practice, LLPs, business corporations, and LLCs may be viable. Although less attractive, general partnerships are an option.

## NEW HAMPSHIRE

Physician/psychologist PCs, LLCs, and employment arrangements with business corporations appear to be the best options in New Hampshire. The professional licensing boards have not yet addressed such arrangements, but as a practical matter, it appears that the state is unlikely to challenge them.

## NEW JERSEY

The PC is a viable vehicle for integrating psychologists' and physicians' practices in New Jersey and is the preferred model at this time. The LLC and business corporation forms are not viable alternatives at present.

## NEW MEXICO

The best options for integrating physician and psychologist practices in New Mexico are the business corporation and the LLC.

## NEW YORK

New York law is very restrictive in this area. At this time, there is no clearly acceptable option for integrating physicians' and psychologists' practices into a single entity. Psychologists may form LLPs and PLLCs with other types of allied mental health professionals. In addition, New York permits networks to be formed only for the purpose of rendering services to a single HMO.

## NORTH CAROLINA

The PC and LLC forms are both advantageous in North Carolina. Both permit psychiatrists and psychologists to provide psychotherapeutic and related services as coowners or employees. Joint partnerships and LLPs also are permitted.

## NORTH DAKOTA

Although it appears unlikely that a joint LLP, PC, or LLC would be challenged in North Dakota, state laws and enforcement policies make this conclusion uncertain. The general partnership remains an option for joint practice.

## OHIO

The ability of physicians and psychologists to practice together in any form in Ohio essentially depends on the Ohio Medical Board's ultimate determination of whether such arrangements constitute impermissible fee splitting. If the board determines that they do not, a registered partnership with limited liability would be the best option (although an argument could be made that business corporations also would be an option).

## OKLAHOMA

The business corporation and PC forms both appear to be attractive options for multidisciplinary practices in Oklahoma. Joint partnerships also are permissible. It is possible, although not certain, that the LLC form also may be used.

## OREGON

The PC and possibly the LLC appear to be the best structures for joint practices of psychologists and physicians. Joint partnerships, and possibly LLPs, also are permissible. It is unclear whether business corporations are viable for this purpose.

## PENNSYLVANIA

Pennsylvania law appears to permit both PCs and LLCs to practice more than one profession, making either an attractive option for joint practice. Partnerships and LLPs also are available for this purpose; it appears that employment of both types of professionals by business corporations is permitted, but this is less certain.

## RHODE ISLAND

Business corporations, and PCs with physician shareholders and psychologist employees, may be viable options for multidisciplinary practices in Rhode Island, but this is not clear. Joint partnerships are permitted.

## SOUTH CAROLINA

A business corporation is not a legally permissible option for multidisciplinary mental health practices in South Carolina, although enforcement of the restrictions appears to be lax. A PC in which both physicians and psychologists hold shares is a viable option. In addition, the routine granting of exceptions under the PLLC law also would make PLLCs an option.

## SOUTH DAKOTA

Employment of physicians and psychologists by a business corporation represents the best option for multidisciplinary practice in South Dakota.

## TENNESSEE

LLPs appear to be the most attractive options for physician-psychologist practices at present, but are subject to whatever conditions the professional licensing authorities may impose. General partnerships also appear to be a permissible option.

## TEXAS

The LLP appears to be the most attractive option at this time.

## UTAH

The best option for multidisciplinary practice in Utah appears to be employment of both types of professionals by a business corporation. The only alternative is employment of psychologists by a physician partnership.

## VERMONT

Under Vermont law a general partnership is the only vehicle for a joint physician/psychologist practice.

## VIRGINIA

PCs and PLLCs are both advantageous forms of organization for joint practices in Virginia. Physicians and psychologists may practice together as coowners or employees in either form. Employment by a business corporation also appears to be permissible, as do partnerships and LLPs.

## WASHINGTON

In Washington a multidisciplinary PC may contract with one or more HMOs for the purpose of providing services to HMO enrollees, but it may not provide services to persons covered by other types of insurance arrangements. No other multidisciplinary vehicles are currently permitted in the state.

## WEST VIRGINIA

The business corporation may be a viable option for joint psychologist/physician practices, if a number of conditions are substantially met. Joint partnerships are permitted. It is unclear whether the LLC form is permissible.

## WISCONSIN

The professional "services corporation" (SC) appears to be the most attractive option for multidisciplinary practices in Wisconsin. Joint partnerships are also permissible.

## WYOMING

The LLC may be a permissible form of integration for physician and psychologist practices in Wyoming, but the unclear language of the LLC statute and the lack of state experience with multidisciplinary professional LLCs create ambiguity. Absent an LLC option, such integrated practices could be general partnerships.

# 3

# Survey of State Laws

THIS CHAPTER PROVIDES *a detailed survey of state laws regarding partnerships, corporations, limited liability corporations, and networks in summary form. Specific guidance from an experienced health care attorney is recommended.*

## ALABAMA

### A. *Partnerships*

An Alabama partnership may be formed to engage in "every trade, occupation, or profession" (Ala. Code § 10-8-2[2]). Neither the partnership laws nor the professional licensing laws of the state impose any limitation on the ability of licensees in different professions to practice together. Psychologists, physicians, and allied health care professionals may practice as partners and employees of a partnership, which may bill for their services.

Alabama does not have an LLP law.

### B. *Corporations*

In two declaratory rulings issued in 1992, the Alabama medical practice authorities approved the employment of physicians by business corporations. Both rulings were addressed to a single business corporation that was seeking approval for its employment of physicians. The Alabama Board of Medical Examiners concluded that "[p]hysicians are free to enter into contracts of employment for their professional service with professional corporations, non-profit corporations, business corporations, partnerships, joint ventures or other entities *provided, however,* that the physician must exercise independent judgment in matters related to the practice of medicine and that his or her actions with respect to the practice of medicine must not be subject to the control of an individual not licensed to practice medicine" (Declaratory Ruling of the Alabama Board of Medical Examiners, October 21, 1992, p. 3). In the other ruling it was held that physician employment did not violate state prohibitions on fee splitting and aiding and abetting the unauthorized practice of medicine (Declaratory Ruling of the Medical Licensure Commission, October 28, 1992). According to Bill Garrett, the assistant attorney general who advises the psychology board, state law does not preclude business corporations from employing psychologists.[8] Thus, provided that the physicians' independent judgment is not infringed upon, it appears that in Alabama a business corporation may employ both physicians and psychologists to render their respective professional services.

Unlike a business corporation, an Alabama professional corporation (PC) is generally limited to the rendition of services "within a single profession" (Ala. Code § 10-4-383). The sole exception is for joint medical/dental PCs. The act also provides that PCs "shall not engage in any other profession other than the profession permitted by its articles of incorporation" (Ala. Code § 10-4-383[b]). Accordingly, a PC cannot be used as a vehicle for the joint practice of physicians and psychologists as either coowners or employees. Ken Dowdy, legal advisor to the Alabama secretary of state, confirmed this conclusion.[9]

## C. LLCs

The Alabama LLC act has a specific provision regulating PLLCs (Ala. Code § 10-12-45). PLLCs may render "only one specific type of professional services," thus precluding physicians and psychologists from practicing as comembers of a PLLC (Ala. Code § 10-12-45[f]). The statute also proscribes a PLLC from engaging in any business other than the one it was organized to render and states that PLLCs are subject to the limitations imposed by the Alabama PC act. As Mr. Dowdy agreed, it is clear that employment of practitioners of a second profession by a PLLC is not permitted under Alabama law.[10]

### D. Networks

Alabama does not regulate preferred provider organizations (PPOs) or provider networks. Psychologists, physicians, and allied health professionals may form and contract with networks in Alabama.

## ALASKA

### A. Partnerships

Alaska's partnership and professional licensing laws do not impose any limitations on the ability of licensees in different professions to practice together (Alaska Stat. § 32.05.010 et seq). Psychologists, physicians, and allied health professionals may practice as partners and employees of a partnership, which may bill for their services.

Alaska does not have an LLP statute.

### B. Corporations

The Alaska business corporation statute indicates that such a corporation may be formed for any lawful purpose other than insurance (Alaska Stat. § 10.06.005). Although the Alaska courts have not considered the issue of corporate practice of medicine, an opinion by the state attorney general provides some support for the view that such practice is barred. At issue was the ability of a foreign professional corporation, organized to practice law, to be granted an Alaska certificate of authority as a foreign *business* corporation (Op. (Inf.) Atty. Gen. Alas., April 16, 1979.) The attorney general relied on the existence of the PC act and the requirement that only licensed persons practice law in the state for his conclusion that business corporations may not practice law. Because identical statutory provisions exist with respect to medical practices, the opinion's reasoning could also be applied in the medical context. However, Assistant Attorney General Ken Truitt, who serves as counsel to the medical and psychology practice boards, indicated that there is no enforcement of such a prohibition at this time.[11] As a practical matter, it appears that a business corporation may employ physicians and psychologists for a mental health practice in Alaska without significant risk of enforcement.

According to the Alaska PC act, a PC "may render one type of professional service only" and may do so only through persons licensed to render the same type of services (Alaska Stat. §§ 10.45.020, 10.45.030). Discussions with regulators revealed uncertainty as to whether medicine and psychology constitute "one type of professional service." Mike Monagle, an attorney with the Banking, Securities and Corporations Division, took the position that the two professions are different types of professional services and that a PC may not practice through both shareholders and employees.[12] On the other hand, Venci Serra, the assistant attorney general who serves as counsel to the same agency, thinks that the two professions might well constitute a single type of service.[13] Given the lack of statutory clarification, it remains uncertain whether the PC form may be used for a joint mental health practice in Alaska.

## C. LLCs

Alaska's LLC act, which took effect July 1, 1995, makes no mention of the provision of professional services. The act permits LLCs to be organized for "any lawful purpose" subject to any other provisions of law to which the activities of the LLC are subject (Alaska Stat. §§ 10.50.010, 10.50.015). Because the relevant licensure laws impose no restrictions on joint practices, the LLC form appears to be available for multidisciplinary mental health practices in Alaska. Mssrs. Monagle and Serra agreed with this conclusion.[14]

## D. Networks

Alaska does not regulate provider networks. Psychologists, physicians, and allied health professionals may form networks and contract with third-party payers to provide services.

## ARIZONA

### A. Partnerships

There do not appear to be any barriers to multidisciplinary partnerships in Arizona. Psychologists, physicians, and allied health professionals may practice as partners and employees of a partnership. The partnership may bill third-party payers for the professional services of its partners and employees.

In 1994 Arizona enacted legislation allowing limited liability partnerships (LLPs) (Ariz. Rev. Stat. Ann. § 29-244 *et seq*). The LLP law does not impose any restrictions on the purposes of an LLP; thus, a multidisciplinary LLP is an option in the state.

## B. *Corporations*

Although the Arizona Supreme Court has not addressed whether a corporation can practice medicine, it has held that the corporate practice of optometry is prohibited in certain circumstances (see *State ex rel. Bd. of Optometry v. Sears, Roebuck & Co.*, 427 P.2d 126 (Ariz. 1967); *Funk Jewelry Co. v. State ex rel. La Prade*, 50 P.2d 945 (Ariz. 1935)). The counsel to the Arizona Board of Medical Examiners indicated that no such prohibition has been enforced in her eight years on the job.[15] However, staff for the Arizona Corporation Commission, which licenses corporations, indicates that it regards the PC form as the only option for a corporation that practices medicine; it would therefore not license a business corporation with the stated purpose of practicing medicine.[16] Whether a corporate practice ban exists in theory or not, it appears that the business corporation option is not available to physicians. On the other hand, the Arizona Corporation Commission takes the view that psychologists may elect to render services as either a business corporation or a PC. The Arizona Board of Psychologist Examiners agrees that there is no legal impediment to the corporate practice of psychology.[17]

The state's professional corporation act limits PCs to the rendition of "one category of professional service" through licensed persons (Ariz. Rev. Stat. Ann. § 10-907).[18] Except for ancillary personnel, only persons licensed to render that particular category of services may serve as shareholders, directors, officers, agents, or employees (Ariz. Rev. Stat. Ann. §§ 10-902(4), 10-903(C)). The commission regards medicine and psychology as two distinct categories of professional services for purposes of the statute.[19] Thus, a physician PC, for example, could neither permit psychologists to hold shares nor hire them as employees to provide psychological services.

As noted above, in the commission's view, psychologists may practice in either a business or a professional corporation. Neither corporate form would permit them to employ physicians, however, owing to prohibitions on the practice of medicine by a business corporation and on multidisciplinary PCs.

## C. LLCs

Professional LLCs, in contrast to PCs, may be organized to render one or more categories of professional services (Ariz. Rev. Stat. Ann. § 29-841(4)). Licensed persons may render their services as members, managers, officers, agents, or employees of a PLLC (Ariz. Rev. Stat. Ann. § 29-844(A)). A PLLC may accordingly render medical, psychological, and allied health services through persons duly licensed in each of those professions.

## D. Networks

Networks of physicians, psychologists, and allied health professionals may thus contract with third-party payers for the provision of services.

## ARKANSAS

### A. Partnerships

There do not appear to be any statutory barriers to multidisciplinary partnerships in Arkansas. Psychologists, physicians, and allied health professionals may practice as partners and employees of a partnership. The partnership may bill third-party payers for the professional services of its partners and employees.

Arkansas law does not provide for LLPs.

### B. Corporations

A business corporation is not a permissible vehicle for the practice of medicine in Arkansas, according to a recent opinion issued by the state attorney general (Op. Atty. Gen. 94-204, 1994)). Although psychologists are not comparably limited, the corporate practice of medicine prohibition would preclude joint physician-psychologist business corporations.

As for PCs, the Arkansas professional corporation act reads in part:

One (1) or more persons duly and properly licensed under and pursuant to the laws of the State of Arkansas to render the same type of professional services, as defined in § 4-29-202,[20] may form a corporation...to own, operate, and maintain a professional corporation and to engage in the professional services thereby authorized by and through its licensed shareholders, directors, officers, and employees only. It is mandatory that such professional services be rendered by or through persons who are duly licensed, individually, to engage in *the profession*. (Ark. Code Ann. § 4-29-206, emphases added).

Although the statutory language is not clear, the highlighted terms appear to prohibit PCs from having shareholders of more than one profession. Ann Purvis, an attorney for the secretary of state, confirms that her office shares this view.[21]

As to licensees for a second profession, an employment relationship with a PC seems permissible. Officers, directors, and shareholders are required to be licensed according to the laws governing "their profession," and no person not so licensed may have any part in the "ownership, management, or control" of the PC (Ark. Code Ann. § 4-19-208). As to employees, by contrast:

Each individual employee licensed pursuant to the laws of this state to engage in *his or her profession* who is employed by a corporation subject to this subchapter shall remain subject to reprimand or discipline for his conduct under the provisions of the laws or regulations governing or applicable to *his or her profession*. (Ark. Code Ann. § 4-19-209, emphases added)

The italicized words—and the fact that the statute distinguishes on this point between owners/managers and employees—imply that licensed persons may practice a second profession as PC employees. Although the act is not explicit on this issue, it appears that a medical PC, for example, could employ psychologists. According to Ms. Purvis, the secretary of state agrees with this interpretation.[22]

## C. LLCs

The Arkansas LLC statute, enacted in 1993, provides that an LLC may not "render professional service within [the] state except through its members, employees of its members, managers, employees and agents who are duly licensed or otherwise legally authorized to render those professional services" (Ark. Code Ann. § 4-32-306). In other words, an LLC may render professional services as long as the services are provided through specified, authorized, and licensed persons. Moreover, neither this provision nor any other in the act imposes a single-specialty limitation.  As a result, an Arkansas LLC may have both physicians and psychologists as members or employees.

## D. Networks

Arkansas does not regulate physician networks or have an independent practice association (IPA) or PPO statute.  Networks of physicians, psychologists, and allied health professionals may contract with third party payers for the provision of services.

## CALIFORNIA

### A. Partnerships

In California psychologists may practice psychology in partnership with other psychologists, and physicians (including psychiatrists) are permitted to practice medicine in partnerships with other physicians (see Cal. Bus. & Prof. Code §§ 2416, 2930.5).  However, if one member of a partnership is a physician, all the members must be physicians.  Thus, multidisciplinary partnerships between psychologists and physicians may not be formed in California.[23]

There is no LLP statute in California.

### B. Corporations

California for-profit business corporations may not employ psychologists, physicians, or other licensed health care professionals (see Cal. Bus. & Prof. Code §§ 2400, 2907).  A nonprofit philanthropic corporation or association providing services to its members may employ psychologists, but it is not clear that such an entity may employ both physicians and psychologists (see 58 Ops. Atty. Gen. 755, Oct. 3, 1975).  However, a California PC may employ practitioners and contract with third-party payers for the services of its employed practitioners (see Cal. Bus. & Prof. Code § 2907.5).  Only licensed individual professionals—not other PCs, business corporations, partnerships, or LLCs—may be shareholders of a California PC.

Under California statutes a PC must be formed primarily to practice a single profession (see Cal. Corp. Code § 13401(b)).  Medicine and psychology are considered different professions.  Nevertheless, multidisciplinary PCs are permissible if they conform with certain restrictions (see Cal. Corp. Code § 13401.5). In addition to psychologists, a psychology PC may have shareholders, officers, directors, and employees who are physicians; podiatrists; nurses; optometrists; marriage, family, or child counselors; clinical social workers; or chiropractors. While a majority of the shares in a psychology PC must be held by psychologists, there is no restriction on the number of physicians or other health care professionals who may be employed by the PC or the ratio of psychologist employees to other professional employees. Conversely, psychologists may be minority shareholders, officers, directors, or employees of PCs formed to practice medicine, podiatry, nursing, counseling, clinical social work, optometry, and chiropractic.

## C. LLCs

In 1994 the California legislature passed an LLC statute. While a chapter was reserved in the bill for provisions regarding PLLCs, no such provisions have been enacted to date (see Cal. S.B. 469 (1994), Chapter 9, p. 97). PLLC provisions may be enacted in the future, but until PLLCs are clearly authorized, this form of organization is not available to psychologists or other professionals in California because of the statute prohibiting "artificial legal entities" (i.e., corporations and LLCs) from practicing professions (Cal. Bus. & Prof. Code § 2400).

## D. Networks

Multidisciplinary networks can operate in California. California law is unusual in that it explicitly permits licensed insurance companies and Blue Cross/Blue Shield plans to enter into preferred provider arrangements (under which insured persons have lower copayments when they receive services from members of a specified panel) and even exclusive provider arrangements (under which the payer makes no payment at all for services rendered by practitioners who are not part of the panel) (see Cal. Ins. Code §§ 10133, 11512, Cal. Code Regs. §2240). The California Department of Corporations (the agency that regulates HMOs in the state) permits HMOs to contract with a nonprofit network for the services of network members as long as the network is managed by practitioners.

# COLORADO

## A. *Partnerships*

In Colorado partnerships may engage in "every trade, occupation, or profession" (Colo. Rev. Stat. Ann. §§ 7-60-106(1), 7-60-102(2)); however, the state's medical practice act says that a physician engages in "unprofessional conduct" by

[1] practicing medicine as the partner, agent, or employee of, or in joint venture with, any person who does not hold a license to practice medicine within this state, or [2] practicing medicine as an employee of, or in joint venture with, any partnership or association any of whose partners or associates do not hold a license to practice medicine within this state, or [3] practicing medicine as an employee of or in joint venture with any corporation other than a professional service corporation for the practice of medicine . . . (Colo. Rev. Stat. Ann. § 12-36-117(1)(m))

Read by itself, the first prohibition would prevent physicians from practicing together as partners with psychologists or as employees of a partnership of psychologists. However, the prohibition must be read in light of the state's 1994 "provider networks" law:

Any provision of [the health professional practice acts] prohibiting the practice of any licensed or certificated health care professional as the partner, agent, or employee of or in joint venture with a person who does not hold a license or certificate to practice such profession within this state shall not apply to professional practice if a professional is participating in a provider network organized pursuant to this part . . . (Colo. Rev. Stat. Ann. § 6-18-303(2))

To meet this "provider network" exception, the professional's independent judgment must be preserved and the professional cannot be required to refer any patient exclusively to a particular provider or supplier.

Several key terms, such as "person" and "joint venture," are not defined. A "provider network," however, is defined broadly as "a group of health care providers formed to provide health care services to individuals (Colo. Rev. Stat. Ann. § 6-18-102(16)). A "provider" is defined as a "state-licensed, state-certified, or state-authorized facility or a practitioner delivering health care services to individuals" (Colo. Rev. Stat. Ann. § 6-18-102(15)). Under these definitions, both physicians and psychologists may form provider networks. Significantly, the statute does not require networks to register with the state; any group that falls within the "provider network" definition may apparently avail itself of the law's protections. Michael Rothman, director of policy at the Colorado Department of Health Care Policy and Financing, indicated that the agency understands the law to be an attempt to allow virtually any relationship among health care providers.[24]

Neither Shannel Lorance, administrative officer of the Colorado State Board of Medical Examiners or Matthew Norwood, the assistant attorney general who represents the board, was aware of the provider networks act before we contacted them.[25] After reviewing the law, Mr. Norwood agreed that it abrogates the first of the prohibitions in the medical practice act (quoted above). Thus, physicians may be partners with other professionals, including psychologists. He noted that the law's failure to address the second or third prohibitions in the medical practice act suggests that those prohibitions remain intact. Since the second prohibition bars physicians from practicing as employees of a partnership that includes nonphysicians, Mr. Norwood concluded that physicians may not practice as employees of a partnership that includes psychologists.

Employment of psychologists by a physician partnership, in contrast, is a viable option. The psychology practice law imposes no prohibition on such employment, and Steve Paull, secretary to the Colorado State Board of Psychologist Examiners, confirmed that such arrangements pose no problem for the board.[26] A physician partnership may therefore employ psychologists in Colorado.

Colorado does not have an LLP statute.

## B. Corporations

A Colorado business corporation may not employ physicians. Under the medical practice act, "unprofessional conduct" by a physician includes "practicing medicine as an employee of or in joint venture with any corporation other than a professional service corporation for the practice of medicine . . . " (Colo. Rev. Stat. Ann. § 12-36-117(1)(m)). Since the new provider networks law does not specifically address this prohibition, it appears to remain in force; Mr. Norwood, counsel to the Colorado State Board of Medical Examiners, shares this view.[27] The statute allowing formation of medical PCs also mandates that, "Except as provided in this section, corporations shall not practice medicine" (Colo. Rev. Stat. Ann. § 12-36-134(7)). A business corporation is thus not an option for joint practices in Colorado.

In contrast to most other states, which have enacted a broadly applicable PC act as part of their corporation laws, Colorado has several profession-specific PC laws in its professional licensing statutes. One allows the formation of PCs for the practice of medicine (Colo. Rev. Stat. Ann. § 12-36-134), and another permits psychology PCs (Colo. Rev. Stat. Ann. § 12-43-211). As to the former, however, "[a]ll shareholders of the corporation shall be persons licensed by the board to practice medicine . . . " (Colo. Rev. Stat. Ann. § 12-36-134(1)(d)). Thus, a physician and a psychologist may not practice as coshareholders of a medical PC. Furthermore, as noted above, the medical PC law also provides that "corporations shall not practice medicine" except in a medical PC (Colo. Rev. Stat. Ann. § 12-36-134(7)). It follows that a psychologist PC may not employ physicians.

The medical PC statute further provides that such a PC "shall be organized solely for the purposes of conducting the practice of medicine only through persons licensed by the board to practice medicine . . . " (Colo. Rev. Stat. Ann. § 12-36-134(1)(b)). This provision rules out the possibility of employing members of a second profession, such as psychologists. Mr. Norwood indicated that the board does not consider such employment arrangements permissible for a medical PC.[28]

## C. LLCs

Colorado's LLC act makes no mention of professional activities. Under the law, an LLC may be organized "for any lawful business, subject to any provisions of law governing or regulating such business within [the] state"; "business" includes "any lawful activity" (Colo. Rev. Stat. Ann. §§7-80-103, 7-80-102(3)). The LLC act thus seems to permit professional LLCs. Under the medical practice law, however, Ms. Lorance, of the Colorado State Board of Medical Examiners, could say only that the availability of LLCs to physicians is an open question; she believes that physician LLCs may already be in existence, but the board has not determined their legality.[29] Even if professional LLCs are permitted, they must be considered in light of the medical practice act's definition of "unprofessional conduct" under Section 12-36-117(1)(m), as modified by the provider networks law in Section 6-18-303(2).

The medical practice act's proscriptions do not refer specifically to LLCs or LLC membership, so the extent to which LLCs come within each proscription's ambit is not clear. As noted, the first prohibition, practicing "as the partner, agent, or employee of, or in joint venture with" an unlicensed person, has been abrogated by the provider networks act. Thus, even if this prohibition applies to comembership in an LLC, it is no longer effective. Physicians and psychologists evidently may practice as comembers of an LLC.

As noted above, however, the second prohibition, on practicing medicine as an employee of or in joint venture with "any partnership or association" with nonphysician members, appears to remain in effect despite the provider networks law. Under this provision, an LLC might well be held to be an "association" within the prohibition's scope; thus, employment of a physician by an LLC with psychologist members is not permissible.

The third prohibition, on practice "in joint venture with any corporation other than a professional service corporation for the practice of medicine" (Colo. Rev. Stat. Ann. § 12-36-117(1)(m)), appears also to have survived enactment of the provider networks law. Since an LLC is not a corporation, a literal reading would not bar physicians from practicing as members of an LLC. Nor would it seem to bar an LLC with physician members from hiring psychologists as employees, since the LLC and licensing statutes do not bar employment of members of a second profession. However, it might also be argued that the clause quoted indicates a legislative intent that medical PCs be the only limited liability vehicle for the practice of medicine. Under this reading, physician LLCs would be barred altogether and thus would not be a vehicle for a multidisciplinary practice.

## D. Networks

As noted earlier, the Colorado provider networks law expressly approves multidisciplinary networks of providers. Psychologists, physicians, and allied health professionals may thus form and contract with networks in the state.

# CONNECTICUT

## A. Partnerships and Professional Associations

There do not appear to be any barriers to multidisciplinary partnerships in Connecticut. Psychologists, physicians, and allied health professionals may practice as partners and employees of a partnership. The partnership may bill third-party payers for the professional services of its partners and employees.

Connecticut's LLP statute took effect January 1, 1996 (1994 Conn. Pub. Act 218). The law does not specifically provide for professional LLPs but imposes no limits on their permissible powers. Joint physician-psychologist LLPs are therefore an option.

Connecticut law also permits the practice of professions by "professional associations" or PAs. However, the statutory authorization of PAs is limited:

[A]ny three or more persons, licensed or authorized to practice *a profession* by the State of Connecticut, may associate to practice *such profession* for profit . . . subject to the laws of the State of Connecticut regulating the practice of *the profession* of the individual members . . . (Conn. Gen. Stat. Ann. § 34-82(1) and (3), emphases added)

The practice of more than one profession by the associates of a Connecticut PA is thus barred. Nothing in the statute, however, precludes the hiring of members of a second profession as PA employees.

## B. Corporations

Connecticut bars the practice of medicine by unlicensed persons (Conn. Gen. Stat. Ann. § 20-9); the state attorney general, interpreting the same provision in a predecessor statute, opined in 1954 that the "implication is clear that the practice of medicine and surgery is restricted to individuals and does not include corporations" (28 Op. Atty. Gen. 248 (1954)).[30] It should be noted, however, that the Connecticut courts have not addressed this issue, and state regulators have indicated that they do not customarily enforce the prohibition.[31] The corporate practice of psychology is not prohibited, according to the Board of Examiners of Psychologists.[32] Although the business corporation form is probably available for a multidisciplinary medical-psychological practice, the fact that the ban on the corporate practice of medicine is still on the books must be noted.

Although in Connecticut a professional corporation may engage in the practice of a profession through employees, multidisciplinary PCs are barred. A PC is defined as a corporation organized

> for the sole and specific purpose of rendering professional service and which has as its shareholders only individuals who themselves are licensed or otherwise legally authorized to render *the same professional service as the corporation.* (Conn. Gen. Stat. Ann. § 33-182a(2), emphasis added)

The act further states that "[a]ny person or group of persons licensed or otherwise legally authorized to render *the same professional services* may organize and become a shareholder or shareholders . . . for the sole and specific purpose of rendering *the same professional service*" (Conn. Gen. Stat. Ann. § 33-182c(a), emphases added). The language of the PC act seems to require that all of a PC's shareholders be licensed in a single profession. The state also takes this position, according to Tom Ryan, legal advisor to the Connecticut secretary of state's office.[33]

A medical PC may not employ psychologists either, because a PC may not "engage in any business other than the rendering of the professional services for which it was specifically incorporated" (Conn. Gen. Stat. Ann. § 33-182f). Mr. Ryan confirmed that the secretary of state shares this view.[34]

## C. LLCs

Connecticut's new LLC law permits the formation of professional LLCs to render professional services (Conn. Gen. Stat. Ann. § 4-100 *et seq.*) Such a PLLC is limited, however, to rendering "only one specific type of professional services and services ancillary to them" (Conn. Gen. Stat. Ann. § 34-119). Although the statute does not define "ancillary," Mr. Ryan indicated that psychological services are not ancillary to medical services, since both medicine and psychology are included in the list of professions in which an LLC may engage (Conn. Gen. Stat. Ann. § 34-101).[35] The formation of a PLLC with both physician and psychologist members is thus not permitted under Connecticut law. Furthermore, a PLLC may not engage in any business other than the single profession for which it was formed. According to Mr. Ryan, this provision forecloses the option of employing members of a second profession.

## D. Networks

Connecticut's only regulation of physician networks is its preferred provider network statute (1993 Conn. Pub. Act 358, amended by 1994 Conn. Pub. Act 235). This law requires registration of physician PPOs, but does not include any provisions relevant to the inclusion of psychologists in a PPO. Networks of physicians, psychologists, and allied health professionals may thus contract with third-party payers for the provision of services.

## DELAWARE

### A. Partnerships

There do not appear to be any barriers to multidisciplinary partnerships in Delaware. The "business" in which a partnership may engage includes "every trade, occupation, or profession" (Del. Code Ann. tit. 6, §§ 1506(a), 1502(2)). Psychologists, physicians, and allied health professionals may practice as partners and employees of a partnership, which may bill for their services.

Delaware's LLP statute similarly imposes no limitations on the permissible purposes or activities of an LLP (Del. Code Ann. tit. 6, § 1544 et seq.). A multidisciplinary practice using the LLP form thus also appears to be an option. George Coyle, the assistant secretary of state who oversees business organization issues, indicated that his office shares these views.[36]

### B. Corporations

Delaware has no statutes or cases proscribing the corporate practice of professions. Malcolm Cobin, the assistant state solicitor who serves as counsel to the Board of Medical Practice and Board of Examiners of Psychologists, indicated that the boards do not prohibit the practice of medicine or psychology by a business corporation.[37] Mr. Coyle agreed that the secretary of state's office also perceives no bar to the corporate employment of professionals, including members of different professions. Thus, it appears that a Delaware business corporation may provide medical and psychological services through its employees.

A Delaware PC may be organized by persons duly licensed to "render the same professional services . . . for the sole and specific purpose of rendering the same professional services" (Del. Code Ann. tit. 8, § 605). Shareholders are limited to those licensed "to render the same professional service as the corporation" (Del. Code Ann. tit. 8, § 603(2)). The statute's wording strongly implies that only single-discipline PCs are permitted. As to employment of members of a second profession, a PC may not "engage in any business other than the rendering of the professional services for which it was specifically incorporated" (Del. Code Ann. tit. 8, § 609). Thus, a PC's provision of a second professional service through employees also appears to be barred. The secretary of state's office does not consider multidisciplinary PCs permissible, according to Mr. Coyle, regardless of whether the second profession is practiced by shareholders or employees.

## C. LLCs

Although the Delaware LLC act makes no specific mention of the provision of professional services by LLCs, it provides that an LLC "may carry on any lawful business, purpose or activity" except insurance and banking (Del. Code Ann. tit. 6, § 18-106(a)). It thus appears that the practice of professions by LLCs is permitted, and nothing in the statute suggests that persons licensed in different professions may not practice as one another's comembers or employees. Since the licensing laws of the medical and psychological professions do not bar multidisciplinary practice arrangements, it appears that the LLC is a viable vehicle for a joint practice in Delaware. The secretary of state's office also has reached this conclusion, according to Mr. Coyle.[38]

## D. Networks

Delaware does not impose any limitations on provider networks. Psychologists, physicians, and allied health professionals may form and contract with networks in Delaware.

# DISTRICT OF COLUMBIA

## A. Partnerships

A District of Columbia partnership may be formed to engage in "every trade, occupation, or profession" (D.C. Code Ann. § 41-101(b)). Neither the partnership laws nor the professional licensing laws impose any limitation on the ability of licensees in different professions to practice together. Psychologists, physicians, and allied health professionals may practice as partners and employees of a partnership, which may bill for their services.

The District's LLP act imposes no limitations on the permissible purposes of an LLP (D.C. Code Ann. § 41-101 *et seq.*). Desiree Jones of the corporations division confirmed that her office accepts LLP filings from professionals, including ones for LLPs that will practice multiple professions.[39] It appears that different types of mental health professionals may practice jointly as partners or employees of an LLP in the District of Columbia.

## B. Corporations

A number of District of Columbia cases, all of which are over 50 years old, have opined that the direct employment of a physician by a business corporation is prohibited (*Group Health Association v. Moor*, 24 F. Supp. 445 (D. D.C., 1938); *U.S. v. American Medical Association*, 110 F.2d 703 (D.C. Cir., 1940), *cert. denied*, 310 U.S. 644 (1940); *Silver v. Lansburgh & Bro.*, 111 F.2d 518 (D.C. Cir., 1940)). However, the District's Board of Medicine has voted that physicians may practice as employees of business coporations.[40] While it must be noted that no court has expressly overturned the prohibition, it thus appears that physician employment by a business corporation is permitted. Inasmuch as the medical and psychology practice acts pose no barrier to joint practices, a business corporation appears to be a suitable vehicle for a multidisciplinary mental health practice in the District of Columbia.

District law defines a PC as a corporation that "has as its shareholders only individuals who themselves are duly licensed to render the same professional service as the corporation" (D.C. Code Ann. § 29-602(1)). The list of professional services contains a number of individual professions (e.g., law, accounting, architecture), but instead of listing physicians and psychologists separately, the definition uses the generic phrase "practitioners of the healing arts" (D.C. Code Ann. § 29-602(2)). This suggests the possibility that all the healing arts are classified as the "same professional service" for purposes of the PC act. Wayne Witkowski, the deputy corporation counsel who advises the corporations division, noted that there is no set policy on this issue but agreed that physicians and psychologists both appear to be "practitioners of the healing arts" who can jointly form a PC.[41] Although District law on this point is not clear, it appears that a multidisciplinary PC of both types of professionals is permitted.

## C. LLCs

The District of Columbia's LLC act appears to permit multidisciplinary PLLCs, although not explicitly. It imports the definition of professional service used in the PC act, but, as noted above, that definition can be read to encompass both medicine and psychology as a single professional service (D.C. Code Ann. §§ 29-1301(25), 29-602(2)). Furthermore, in contrast to the PC act, the LLC act does not impose an explicit single-profession requirement on PLLCs. Mr. Witkowski confirmed that multiple-profession PLLCs seem to be permissible under the act.[42] Accordingly, it appears that a PLLC may be formed by physicians and psychologists and that they may render their respective professional services as comembers or employees.

## D. Networks

The District of Columbia does not regulate provider networks. Psychologists, physicians, and allied health professionals may form networks and contract with third-party payers to provide services.

## FLORIDA

### A. Partnerships

There do not appear to be any statutory barriers to multidisciplinary partnerships in Florida. Psychologists, physicians (including psychiatrists), and allied health professionals may practice as partners and employees of a partnership. The partnership may bill third-party payers for the professional services of its partners and employees. All of the typical advantages and disadvantages to practicing in a partnership would apply to partnerships in Florida. There is no LLP statute in Florida.

## B. *Corporations*

In 1987 the Florida Board of Medicine clearly stated in a formal published opinion that a business corporation may employ, and bill for the services of, physicians. Thus, there is no prohibition on the corporate practice of medicine in Florida (see *In re* Petition of John W. Lister, M.D., 9 FALR 6299, Fla. Bd. of Med., 1987). While the Florida Board of Psychology has not issued an analogous opinion, there are no explicit prohibitions on the corporate practice of psychology in Florida statutes. Moreover, there is no restriction on a single-business corporation employing psychologists, physicians, and allied health professionals (except dentists and optometrists for whom there are specific statutory provisions). Thus, in Florida a multidisciplinary practice may be established relatively easily by simply incorporating a business corporation.

Florida statutes authorize PCs, but they must be formed "for the sole and specific purpose of rendering the same and specific professional service" (see Fla. Stat. Ann. § 621.05). Thus, a PC may be formed to render either psychology services or the professional services of physicians but not to render the services of both psychologists and physicians. Only individual psychologists, psychology PCs, and psychology PLLCs may be shareholders of a psychology PC. Multidisciplinary PCs clearly are not permitted in Florida.

## C. LLCs

Florida's LLC statute neither explicitly authorizes nor prohibits the practice of professions by standard LLCs (i.e., LLCs that are not PLLCs). It was not possible to locate any decisions by Florida courts or regulatory agencies that address this issue. However, the LLC statute gives LLCs all of the powers that are held by individuals to carry out their business and affairs (see Fla. Stat. Ann. § 608.404). Since individuals may practice psychology or medicine, it would appear that a standard LLC may practice each of these professions by hiring licensed professionals and billing third-party payers for their services. Moreover, since an individual may be dually licensed in both of these professions and practice both, a standard LLC may have both psychologist and physician members and employees. Finally, since business corporations are authorized to practice psychology, medicine, and most allied health professions in Florida, it would be inconsistent to prohibit standard LLCs from engaging in the same activities.

Standard LLCs would appear to be a viable vehicle for multidisciplinary practices in Florida.

Florida is one of the minority of states in which LLCs are subject to the same state tax laws as corporations (see Fla. Stat. Ann. § 608.471).

PLLCs may be organized in Florida by psychologists (see Fla. Stat. Ann. § 621.051); however, like PCs, they may only be formed for the specific purpose of rendering the services of a single profession. Thus, PLLCs cannot be used for multidisciplinary practices.

## D. Networks

Psychologists, physicians, and allied health professionals may form and contract with networks in Florida. In turn, Florida networks may contract with all types of third-party payers. However, the Florida Department of Insurance has the authority to review contracts involving HMOs and to cancel a contract if the rates paid by the HMO are determined to be excessive (see Fla. Stat. Ann. § 641.234(2)).

## GEORGIA

### A. Partnerships and Professional Associations

There do not appear to be any statutory barriers to multidisciplinary partnerships in Georgia. Psychologists, physicians, and allied health professionals may practice as partners and employees of a partnership. The partnership may bill third-party payers for the professional services of its partners and employees.

LLPs may not be created under Georgia law, but the state certifies foreign LLPs (i.e., LLPs organized under the laws of another state; see Ga. Code Ann. § 14-8-45). The laws of the state in which the LLP was formed generally govern the LLP. Georgia requires all foreign LLPs to maintain liability insurance in the amount of at least $1 million (see Ga. Code Ann. § 14-8-44). Thus, if the laws of the state where an LLP was formed permit it to be a multidisciplinary practice, it may render services in the fields of psychology, medicine, and other professions in Georgia through partners and employees who are licensed to practice those professions in Georgia.

Georgia law authorizes professionals to practice together in a professional association. A PA is similar to a partnership except that its members are not personally liable for the business debts of the association unless they consent to beforehand. However, a PA may only render one type of professional service; thus, PAs are not a viable structure for a multidisciplinary practice (see Ga. Code Ann. §§ 14-10-3, 14-10-5, 1963 Op. Atty. Gen., at 791).

## B. Corporations

Georgia's professional licensing statutes have been interpreted to prohibit business corporations from practicing learned professions, including psychology and medicine. Both the Georgia Board of Examiners of Psychologists and the Board of Medical Examiners have statutory authority to request that a court enjoin corporations from practicing these professions (see Ga. Code Ann. §§ 43-34-43, 43-39-18).

Georgia statutes authorize PCs, but they must be formed to practice only a single profession (e.g., medicine or psychology; see Ga. Code Ann. § 14-7-4). A PC's shareholders must all be professionals who are licensed in a single profession and who actively practice in the PC (see Ga. Code Ann. § 14-7-5). PCs thus do not appear to be a feasible structure for multidisciplinary practice in Georgia.

## C. LLCs

Georgia LLCs are explicitly permitted to employ professionals and to bill for their services (see Ga. Code Ann. § 14-11-1107(f)). The members and managers of a Georgia LLC may be individuals, partnerships, business corporations, PCs, or other LLCs (see Ga. Code Ann. §§ 14-11-101(2),(5),(15),(16),(19)).

There are no statutory barriers to an LLC being a multidisciplinary practice in Georgia. There are no requirements that the professional members, managers, employers, or subcontractors of a Georgia LLC all have the same license. It thus appears that LLCs may employ or contract with, and bill for the services of, psychologists, psychiatrists and other physicians, and allied health professionals.

Georgia's LLC statute does not have any PLLC provisions.

## D. Networks

Psychologists, physicians, and allied health professionals may form and contract with networks in Georgia. In turn, Georgia networks may contract with all types of payers, including insurers, Blue Cross/Blue Shield plans, and HMOs (see Ga. Code Ann. §§ 33-30-22(6), 33-30-23(a)). However, a network must file with the Georgia commissioner of insurance information describing its activities and contracts if it contracts with any payer other than a self-insured employer, even if it does not engage in the business of insurance (see Ga. Code Ann. § 33-30-23(d)).

# HAWAII

## A. Partnerships

Hawaii's partnership law imposes no limitations on the permissible purposes of a general partnership (see  Haw. Rev. Stat. §§ 425-1 *et seq.*). Neither the partnership laws nor the professional licensing laws impose any limitation on the ability of licensees in different professions to practice together.  Psychologists, physicians, and allied health professionals may practice as partners and employees of a partnership, which may bill for their services.

Hawaii does not have an LLP statute.

## B. Corporations

Hawaii's business corporation law provides that "[e]very corporation incorporated under this chapter has the purpose of engaging in any lawful business, other than . . . carrying on any profession, except pursuant to [the PC act] . . . " (Haw. Rev. Stat. § 415-3).  Thus, it is clear that the PC is the only form of corporation that may provide professional services in Hawaii and that the business corporation is not a viable form or organization for a multidisciplinary practice.

According to Hawaii's PC act:

A professional corporation may be incorporated for the purpose of rendering professional services within two or more professions, and for any purpose or purposes for which corporations may be organized under the Hawaii Business Corporation Act . . . to the extent that any combination of professional purposes or of professional and business purposes is permitted by the licensing laws and rules of this State applicable to the professions. (Haw. Rev. Stat. § 415A-3(b))

Constance Cabral, executive officer of Hawaii's Board of Medical Examiners, indicated that the board has not adopted a position on physician-psychologist PCs but that it would not act to prevent such a combination.[43] James Kobashigawa, executive officer of the Board of Psychology, indicated that the same situation prevailed with respect to his board.[44] Lauren Namba of the state's Department of Business Regulation, which receives corporate filings, indicated that the department would accept for filing a PC's articles of incorporation indicating that it would render services in both professions.[45] It thus appears that a multidisciplinary PC is a viable option in Hawaii.

## C. LLCs

Hawaii law does not provide for LLCs.

## D. Networks

Hawaii does not regulate provider networks. Psychologists, physicians, and allied health professionals may form networks and contract with third-party payers to provide services.

## IDAHO

## A. Partnerships

In Idaho a partnership may be formed to engage in "every trade, occupation, or profession" (Idaho Code § 53-302). Neither the partnership laws nor the professional licensing laws impose any limitation on the ability of licensees in different professions to practice together. Psychologists, physicians, and allied health professionals may practice as partners and employees of a partnership, which may bill for their services.

Idaho's LLP act took effect July 1, 1995 (Idaho Code § 53-543A). The law does not impose any restrictions on multidisciplinary professional LLPs, so the LLP form is a viable option for such practice.

## B. Corporations

In Idaho a business corporation may not employ physicians. The state's business corporation law provides that, where the law makes special provision for corporations that serve a particular purpose, the corporation must be organized under that special law rather than the general act (Idaho Code § 30-1-3). Idaho does include such "special provisions" for corporations organized to provide professional services, and the PC law specifies that psychologists and physicians are among the professionals who may avail themselves of the PC form (Idaho Code § 30-1303(1)). Consequently, any corporation offering professional services must be organized as a PC, not as a business corporation to employ professionals. Everett Wohlers, deputy secretary of state for commercial affairs, confirmed this interpretation of the law.[46]

Under Idaho's professional services corporation act, PCs may be organized "for the sole and specific purpose of rendering the same and specific professional service or allied professional services" (Idaho Code § 30-1304). Both medicine and psychology are "professional services" (Idaho Code § 30-1303(1)); "allied professional services" are "professional services which are so related in substance that they are frequently offered in conjunction with one another as parts of the same service package to the consumer" (Idaho Code § 30-1303(3)). The authorization of PCs to offer allied professional services, however, specifically does not extend to situations in which "the laws of [the] state pertaining to specific professions or the codes of ethics or professional responsibility of any of the professions involved in such a proposed combination prohibit such a combination of professional services" (Idaho Code § 30-1304). Nancy Herr, of the Idaho Board of Medicine, indicated that her board, as well as the Board of Psychologist Examiners, has approved the physician-psychologist combination.[47]

Idaho law further states that a PC may not engage in any business other than the rendering of the professional services for which it was specifically incorporated (Idaho Code § 30-1307). According to Mr. Wohlers, however, the fact that the relevant practice boards have approved physician-psychologist combinations means that either type of professional may serve as an employee of a PC owned by the other type of professional.[48] It thus appears that in Idaho a medical PC could also engage psychologists as employees and that a psychology PC could have physician employees.

## C. LLCs

Idaho law expressly provides for professional LLCs. A PLLC, like a PC, may have members who are licensed in different "allied professional services," which are defined identically as in the PC statute (Idaho Code § 53-615). Since the relevant professional boards have approved joint practice by physicians and psychologists, such professionals may practice as coowners or employees of a PLLC on the same basis as if it were a PC. Mr. Wohlers confirmed this conclusion.[49]

### D. Networks

Idaho does not regulate provider networks. Psychologists, physicians, and allied health professionals may form networks and contract with third-party payers to provide services.

## ILLINOIS

### A. Partnerships and Professional Associations

Physicians may not practice as partners of nonphysicians in Illinois. Under the state's medical practice act, it is grounds for disciplinary action for a physician to

> [divide] with anyone other than physicians with whom the licensee practices in a partnership, Professional Association, limited liability company, or Medical or Professional Corporation any fee, commission, rebate or other form of compensation for any professional services not actually and personally rendered. (225 Ill. Comp. Stat. Ann. § 60/22(A)(14))

Helene Hoffman, general counsel to the Illinois Department of Professional Regulation (and to the professional practice boards), explained that the department interprets the provision to mean that physicians may not practice as partners or employees (or as coowners in the other corporate forms named) of nonphysicians.[50] Since LLPs are another form of partnership, the same prohibition applies to them. Ms. Hoffman explained, however, that employment of nonphysicians by a physician partnership does not constitute impermissible fee splitting. Thus, a joint mental health practice could be carried on by a physician partnership (either general or LLP) with psychologist employees.

Illinois law also permits the formation of "professional associations" or

PAs. However, the physician fee-splitting ban extends to PAs; so physicians and nonphysicians may not be coowners of a PA.[51]  In addition, under the PA statute, "[e]xcept for an association formed for the purpose of rendering professional services within the fields of medicine, dentistry and nursing, no professional association organized pursuant to this Act shall engage in more than one type of professional service" (805 Ill. Comp. Stat. Ann. § 305/1).  Since psychology is not listed, the provision of both medical and psychological services by a single PA, including through employees, is barred.  Pat Zander of the secretary of state's office confirmed this conclusion.[52]

## B. Corporations

A prohibition on the practice of medicine by a business corporation is enforced in Illinois.  A similar law is found in a 1953 opinion of the attorney general, enforcing the doctrine, and two cases from the 1930s barring the corporate practice of dentistry (Op. Atty. Gen. No. 26 (May 12, 1953); *Dr. Allison, Dentist, Inc. v. Allison*, 196 N.E. 799 (Ill. 1935); *People v. United Medical Service*, 200 N.E. 157 (Ill. 1936)).  Relying on these decisions, the secretary of state denies incorporation to business corporations whose purposes include the provision of medical services through employees.  Ms. Zander confirmed that this is her office's position.[53]

The state's psychology practice act permits licensure of associations, partnerships, and corporations as well as individuals (225 Ill. Comp. Stat. Ann. § 15/3(a)).  However, the law specifies that no license shall be issued to a corporation "the stated purpose of which includes or which practices or which holds itself out as available to practice clinical psychology" unless it is organized under the PC act (225 Ill. Comp. Stat. Ann. § 15/3(b)).  The employment of psychologists by a business corporation is therefore precluded.

Under the Illinois medical practice act's fee-splitting prohibition, physicians may not be PC shareholders with persons not licensed as physicians (225 Ill. Comp. Stat. Ann. § 60/22(A)(14)).  The PC act independently precludes such arrangements.  A PC is defined as a corporation organized

> solely for the purpose of rendering one category of professional service or related professional services and which has as its shareholders, directors, officers, agents and employees (other than ancillary

personnel) only individuals who are duly licensed by [the] State . . .
to render that particular category of professional service or related
professional services . . . (805 Ill. Comp. Stat. Ann. § 10/3.4(a))

The definition of "professional service" embraces both medicine and psychology, since it includes any personal service for which a license is required (805 Ill. Comp. Stat. Ann. § 10/3.5). Illinois law mandates that
only certain combinations of professions are "related"; medicine and psychology are not among the ones listed (805 Ill. Comp. Stat. Ann. § 10/
3.6). Thus, it is clear that an Illinois PC may neither have physicians and
psychologists as coshareholders, nor engage members of a second profession as employees. Ms. Zander reported that her office concurs with this
conclusion.[54]

Another vehicle for the provision of professional medical services in
Illinois is the "medical corporation." An MC may be formed for the following purposes:

to own, operate and maintain an establishment for the study, diagnosis and treatment of human ailments and injuries, whether physical or mental, and to promote medical, surgical and scientific re-
search or knowledge . . . (805 Ill. Comp. Stat. Ann. § 15/2)

Because all the officers, directors, and shareholders must be licensed physicians, psychologists could not be coowners of an MC (805 Ill. Comp.
Stat. Ann. § 15/13). Such an arrangement would also violate the medical
fee-splitting law (225 Ill. Comp. Stat. Ann. § 60/22(A)(14)). Unlike the
state's PC Act, however, its MC act does not explicitly extend the single-
specialty restriction to employees of the entity; it requires employees to be
licensed physicians only if they give "medical or surgical treatment, consultation or advice . . . " (805 Ill. Comp. Stat. Ann. § 15/2). However, as
noted above, the only corporations for which the psychology practice act
allows licensees to render services are those formed under the PC act (225
Ill. Comp. Stat. Ann. § 15/3(b)). Since MCs are formed under a statute
other than the PC act, it follows that psychologists may not practice as
employees of an MC.

## C. LLCs

The Illinois LLC Act expressly prohibits LLCs from engaging in the
practice of medicine unless "all the members and managers are licensed to

practice medicine" (805 Ill. Comp. Stat. Ann. § 180/1-25(4)). LLCs with physicians and psychologists as co-members are thus clearly prohibited. However, the statute does not address employment relationships, and as was discussed above, the physician fee-splitting statute appears not to preclude a physician-owned entities from employing licensees in a second profession. It thus appears that a joint practice may be accomplished by having psychologists as employees of a physician LLC.

### D. Networks

Illinois law requires that PPOs register with the state's insurance department but does not impose any restrictions on the makeup of provider networks (215 Ill. Comp. Stat. Ann. § 5/370f et seq.). Psychologists, physicians, and allied health professionals may form and contract with networks in the state.

## INDIANA

### A. Partnerships

Indiana law permits partnerships to engage in "every trade, occupation or profession" and appears to not pose any barriers to multidisciplinary partnerships (Ind. Code § 23-4-1-2). Psychologists, physicians, and allied health professionals may practice as partners and employees of a partnership. The partnership may bill third-party payers for the professional services of its partners and employees.

Indiana's LLP act took effect October 1, 1995 (Ind. Code § 23-4-1-44 et seq.). Inasmuch as it imposes no limitations on the permissible purposes of an LLP, the LLP appears to be a viable form for a multidisciplinary mental health practice in Indiana.

### B. Corporations

Under Indiana's medical practice act, health care organizations whose members, shareholders, or partners are authorized to provide services in any of a number of health professions may employ physicians without engaging in the unlawful practice of medicine (Ind. Code § 25-22.5-1-2(c)). The organization may not, however, "direct or control [the] independent medical acts, decisions, or judgment of [a] licensed physician." The statute does not address particular forms of practice organization, such as business corporations; it would apply to a business corporation only if the shareholders were licensed health professionals.

In a 1938 case the Indiana Supreme Court affirmed the state's prohibition on the employment of physicians by a business corporation (*Iterman v. Baker*, 15 N.E.2d 365, Ind. 1938). The court has not revisited the issue. In 1987, however, the Indiana Court of Appeals suggested that, in light of changing circumstances and the enactment of the state's professional corporation act, the doctrine was no longer reasonable (*Sloan v. Metropolitan Health Council of Indianapolis, Inc.*, 516 N.E.2d 1104, Ind. Ct. App. 1987). However, the latter case did not overrule the former (nor could it, because it was decided by a lower court). The director of the Medical Liscensing Board of Indiana indicated that the board has not considered the issue recently and thus cannot provide any guidance on the vitality of the corporate practice ban or its interaction with the statute discussed above.[55] Nate Feltman, counsel to the secretary of state, indicated that the secretary of state's office does consider business corporations to be barred from the practice of professions and that it would reject the filing of a business corporation if the filing identified professional practice as a corporate purpose.[56] In this climate of uncertainty a business corporation may well choose to employ physicians to practice medicine; however, until *Iterman* is overruled, the prohibition must be regarded as creating some legal risk for such arrangements.

In Indiana one or more licensed health care professionals may form a PC to render their professional services (Ind. Code § 23-1.5-2-3(a)(4)). The statutory definition of health care professional expressly includes both physicians and psychologists, so both may own PC shares; the exclusion of other allied mental health professionals from the list, however, suggests that they are limited to employment (rather than shareholder) relationships (Ind. Code § 23-1.5-1-8). Nothing in the statute precludes a PC from rendering more than one type of health care professional service through licensed persons (Ind. Code § 23-1.5-2-5(a)). Mr. Feltman indicated that the secretary of state's office does not consider multidisciplinary groups to be barred, and the relevant professional licensure boards share this view.[57] Thus, a PC whose shareholders or employees practice both medicine and psychology is an option in Indiana.

## C. LLCs

An Indiana LLC may be organized and may conduct business "for any lawful purpose" subject to any statutes regulating the business (Ind. Code § 23-18-2-1). An LLC may provide professional services to the extent authorized by the licensing authority (Ind. Code § 23-18-2-2(15)). The LLC law uses the PC act's definition of "professional services," which include both physician and psychologist services (Ind. Code §§ 23-1.5-1-11(4), 23-1.5-1-8). The statute expressly states that it is not intended to regulate the provision of professional services or otherwise interfere with the authority of professional licensing authorities (Ind. Code § 23-18-2-3). Again, neither the secretary of state nor the practice boards object to joint physician/psychologist LLCs.[58] Thus, multidisciplinary LLCs are an option under Indiana law.

## D. Networks

Indiana has a PPO statute, but it requires only a filing by the PPO and does not suggest any limits on multidisciplinary networks (Ind. Code § 27-8-11-5). Networks of physicians, psychologists, and allied health professionals may thus contract with third-party payers for the provision of their services.

## IOWA

## A. Partnerships

An Iowa partnership may be formed to engage in "every trade, occupation, or profession" (Iowa Code § 486.2). Neither the partnership laws nor the professional licensing laws impose any limitations on the ability of licensees in different professions to practice together. Psychologists, physicians, and allied health professionals may practice as partners and employees of a partnership, which may bill for their services.

Iowa's LLP act imposes no limitations on the permissible purposes of an LLP (Iowa Code § 486.44 et seq.). Monte Bratelli, an attorney for the corporations division of the secretary of state's office, indicated that the issue has not arisen but that his office would see no reason to prohibit a multidisciplinary professional LLP.[59] It thus appears that in Iowa different types of mental health professionals may conduct a joint practice as partners or employees of an LLP.

## B. *Corporations*

In a 1931 case the Iowa Supreme Court implicitly upheld the state's prohibition on the corporate practice of medicine, affirming an injunction barring an individual who owned a corporation from continuing to cause the corporation to employ physicians (*State v. Baker*, 212 Iowa 571, 235 N.W. 313, 1931). Other opinions issued between 1931 and 1973 applied the prohibition on corporate practice with respect to other professions, and in 1954 the attorney general affirmed the doctrine's application to physicians (1954 Op. Atty. Gen. 122). In 1991, however, the attorney general revisited the issue and, after surveying prior case law, concluded that the prohibition was no longer in effect (1991 Iowa A.G. Lexis 25, July 12, 1991). The attorney general adopted the position that there is not a general bar to corporate employment of physicians but only to "improper dominion and control" over professional practice (1991 Iowa A.G. Lexis, at 12, 13).

In conclusion, the opinion stated that, "unless prohibited by statute or by public policy considerations against lay control of medical judgment and lay exploitation of the practice of medicine, corporations organized and controlled by non-physicians, may provide medical services to the public through employed physicians." Because the medical and psychology laws do not prohibit multidisciplinary practice arrangements, it appears that members of the two professions may practice jointly as employees of a business corporation as long as the corporation does not exercise control over the physicians' medical judgment. Deputy Attorney General Julie Pottorff, who advises the Iowa's Board of Medical Examiners, and Deputy Attorney General Maureen McGuire, who advises the state's Board of Psychology Examiners, indicated that their respective boards had not addressed this question directly, but they did not disagree with the conclusion stated above.[60]

In Iowa a PC may be organized to practice a single profession or "two or more specific professions which could lawfully be practiced in combination by a licensed individual or a partnership of licensed individuals" (Iowa Code § 496C.4). Neither the state's PC act nor the medical and psychology practice acts specifically address what combinations are lawful. Ms. Pottorff and Ms. McGuire indicated that their respective practice boards have not addressed the issue but that they are unaware of any reasons why the boards might reject a physician- psychologist combination.[61] Mr. Bratelli indicated that the secretary of state would accept such a PC's articles of incorporation. Thus, it seems likely that a multidisciplinary PC of physicians and psychologists would be permitted in Iowa.[62]

## C. LLCs

Like its PC law, Iowa's PLLC law permits otherwise lawful combinations of professions (Iowa Code § 490A.1502). The attorneys for the practice boards and the secretary of state expressed the same views as for PCs (discussed above).[63] It thus appears probable that an Iowa PLLC may be formed by physicians and psychologists to render both types of services.

## D. Networks

Iowa does not regulate provider networks. Psychologists, physicians, and allied health professionals may form networks and contract with third-party payers to provide services.

## KANSAS

### A. Partnerships

A Kansas partnership may be formed to engage in "every trade, occupation, or profession" (Kan. Stat. Ann. § 56-302(b)). Neither the partnership laws nor the professional licensing laws prevent licensees in different professions from practicing together. Psychologists, physicians, and allied health professionals may practice as partners and employees of a partnership, which may bill for their services.

A recently enacted law provides that LLPs have the same powers as general partnerships (Kan. Stat. Ann. § 56-347). The LLP thus is another option for multidisciplinary practices in Kansas.

### B. Corporations

The Kansas Supreme Court has reaffirmed the state's prohibition on the employment of physicians by a business corporation, holding that the PC form is the only corporate option available for medical practice (*Early Detection Ctr., Inc. v. Wilson*, 811 P.2d 860, Kan. 1991). Though the court recently declined to extend the prohibition to physician employment by a nonprofit charitable hospital, it did not disturb the earlier holding (*St. Francis Regional Med. Ctr., Inc. v. Weiss*, 869 P.2d 606, Kan. 1994). Employment by a business corporation is therefore not a viable option for a joint physician/psychologist practice in Kansas.

The general rule in Kansas is that PCs are limited to rendering a single type of professional service; medicine and psychology each constitute one type (Kan. Stat. Ann. §§ 17-2710, 17-2707(b)). The PC act, however, makes an exception for combinations of certain types of professionals, and medicine and psychology are among those listed. A PC must obtain certificates from the regulatory boards of any profession whose services the PC might render, indicating that the incorporators are duly licensed (Kan. Stat. Ann. § 17-2709). If this is done, a Kansas PC may be used as a vehicle for multidisciplinary practice by physicians and psychologists, as either coowners or employees. This conclusion was confirmed by Chad Tenpenny of the secretary of state's office.[64]

## C. LLCs

Kansas LLCs may exercise all powers that PCs may exercise and are "limited to the practice of one profession, except as provided in K.S.A. 17-2710 and amendments thereto" (Kan. Stat. Ann. § 17-7604(q)). As noted above, the statute permits joint physician/psychologist practices. Mr. Tenpenny agreed that such multidisciplinary practices are an option for LLCs.[65]

## D. Networks

Kansas does not regulate provider networks. Psychologists, physicians, and allied health professionals may form and contract with networks in the state.

## KENTUCKY

## A. Partnerships

There do not appear to be any barriers to multidisciplinary partnerships in Kentucky. A partnership may be formed to carry on a business, and it is specified that "business" includes "every trade, occupation, or profession" (Ky. Rev. Stat. Ann. § 362.155). No provision in the partnership statute limits professional partnerships to a single profession. Psy-

chologists, physicians, and allied health professionals may practice as partners and employees of a partnership. The partnership may bill third-party
payers for the professional services of its partners and employees.

LLPs are permitted in Kentucky and may have the same powers as
general partnerships (Ky. Rev. Stat. Ann. § 362.575). Thus, multidisciplinary LLPs are an option in the state.

## B. *Corporations*

There is no law in Kentucky regarding the employment of physicians
by business corporations. Wes Faulkner, counsel to the Kentucky Board of
Medical Licensure, confirmed that the issue is not addressed by Kentucky
statutes, regulations, or cases.[66] Business corporations may be formed to
engage in any lawful business, subject to any statutory provisions regulating the business (Ky. Rev. Stat. Ann. § 271B.3-010). Since there are no
provisions prohibiting the practice of medicine by a corporation, medical
practice by a business corporation's shareholder or by employee physicians
seems to be permissible. Neither is there a ban on the corporate practice
of psychology, leading to the same conclusion for psychologists. Since, as
noted below, there also is no law barring multidisciplinary practices, it
appears that a joint physician/psychologist business corporation is permitted in the state.

Kentucky's professional services corporation statute limits PCs in the
following way:

> One or more individuals, each of whom is licensed to render related
> professional services such that applicable licensing laws and regula-
> tions would not prohibit the practice of such multiple professional
> services through a single business partnership, may incorporate and
> form a professional service corporation . . . (Ky. Rev. Stat. Ann.
> § 274.015(1))

The attorneys who serve as counsels to the Kentucky Boards of Medical
Licensure and Psychology have indicated that there are no licensing laws
or regulations barring multidisciplinary practice arrangements.[67] The statute further provides that a PC may not "engage in any business other than
the rendering of the professional service or services for which it was incorporated . . . " (Ky. Rev. Stat. Ann. § 274.115). It therefore appears that in

Kentucky physicians and psychologists may practice jointly as shareholders of a PC incorporated to render both types of service; however, a PC incorporated for the purpose of rendering only one type of professional service many not employ members of a second profession.

## C. LLCs

A Kentucky LLC may be organized for any lawful purpose "including the provision of one (1) or more professional services" (Ky. Rev. Stat. Ann. § 275.005). The services of both physicians and psychologists are considered "professional services" (Ky. Rev. Stat. Ann. § 275.015(19)). Even so, the LLC remains subject to the authority of relevant regulatory boards, including any limits on the provision of multiple professional services (Ky. Rev. Stat. Ann. § 275.010). As noted above, the medical and psychology practice boards do not impose any such restrictions; thus, both categories of professionals may practice as members or employees of an LLC.

## D. Networks

Kentucky's PPO regulation does not address the composition of the provider panel of a PPO or network (806 Ky. Admin. Regs. 18:020). Networks of physicians, psychologists, and allied health professionals may contract with third-party payers for the provision of services.

## LOUISIANA

## A. Partnerships

Louisiana law does not restrict the permissible purposes of a partnership (La. C.C. art. 2801 et seq.). Neither the partnership laws nor the professional licensing laws impose any limitations on the ability of licensees in different professions to practice together. Psychologists, physicians, and allied health professionals may practice as partners and employees of a partnership, which may bill for their services.

The Louisiana LLP act imposes no limitations on the permissible purposes of an LLP (La. Rev. Stat. Ann. § 9:3432 et seq.). It appears that different types of mental health professionals may therefore conduct a joint practice as partners or employees of an LLP. Clay Wertz, an attorney for the secretary of state, agreed with this conclusion, as did Robert Conrad, Jr., a private attorney who acts as counsel to the Louisiana Board of Medical Examiners, and Jim Quillen, chairman of the state's Board of Examiners of Psychologists.[68]

## B. *Corporations*

Louisiana's Board of Medical Examiners has opined that the employment of physicians by a business corporation is not per se violative of the state's medical practice act (Statement of Position, Louisiana State Board of Medical Examiners, September 24, 1992). The board noted that a particular employment relationship might well run afoul of the law if a corporate employer controlled or directed a physician's provision of services or otherwise "undermine[d] the essential incidents of the physician-patient relationship." As long as the physician's independence is preserved, however, employment by a business corporation is permitted. There is no bar to psychologists practicing with physicians, as the relevant professional board personnel confirmed. Mssrs. Conrad and Quillen confirmed that it thus appears physicians and psychologists may practice together as employees of a business corporation.[69]

Louisiana law provides for a number of profession-specific corporate vehicles, including ones for medical and psychological professionals. A professional medical corporation (PMC) may be formed by individual medical licensees (La. Rev. Stat. Ann. § 12:902). In contrast to many states, Louisiana does not require that all shares be held by licensed physicians; however, unlicensed shareholders "shall have no voting rights for any purpose whatever, shall not participate in the corporation's earnings, and shall have no access to any records or communications pertaining to medical services rendered by, or any other affairs of, the corporation" (La. Rev. Stat. Ann. § 12:905(B)). Furthermore, PMCs "shall engage in no business other than the practice of medicine" (La. Rev. Stat. Ann. § 12:904). Even though technically psychologists may hold shares in a PMC, it is apparent that they may not practice their profession as shareholders or employees of the PMC. Mr. Wertz confirmed that PMCs are not an option for joint practice in Louisiana.[70]

Professional psychology corporations (PPCs) are subject to virtually identical restrictions. Shareholders not licensed as psychologists are subject to the same limitations described above, and PPCs may not engage in any business other than the practice of psychology (La. Rev. Stat. Ann. §§

12:1134(B), 12:1133). The PPC form is accordingly not available for a joint medical/psychological practice.

## C. LLCs

In Louisiana LLCs may conduct business, in any profession, for any lawful purpose, with certain exceptions not relevant here (La. Rev. Stat. Ann. §§ 12:1302(A), 12:1301(2)). This general rule is subject to the provisions that LLCs may not be formed if prohibited by other state law and that they remain subject to any limitations such law imposes (La. Rev. Stat. Ann. § 12:1302(B)). Pursuant to a 1995 amendment, however, the LLC act makes specific provision for dental PLLCs, without comparable provisions for any other profession (La. Rev. Stat. Ann. § 12:981(B)). Mr. Wertz noted that the secretary of state's office still considers LLCs permissible for other professions.[71] As for multiprofession LLCs, he noted that, while no formal policy is yet in place, the office would accept articles for filing in the absence of any prohibition in the medical and psychology practice acts. Although it cannot be stated with certainty, it appears that a Louisiana LLC may carry on such a practice. Personnel at the professional practice boards also took this view.[72]

## D. Networks

Louisiana law specifically provides that both physicians and psychologists may be included in PPOs (La. Rev. Stat. Ann. § 40:2202(6)). Psychologists, physicians, and allied health professionals may form networks and contract with third-party payers to provide services.

## MAINE

## A. Partnerships

There do not appear to be any barriers to multidisciplinary partnerships in Maine. Psychologists, physicians, and allied health professionals may practice as partners and employees of a partnership. A partnership may bill third-party payers for the professional services of its partners and employees.

Maine law does not provide for LLPs.

### B. *Corporations*

In Maine, a business corporation may be organized to carry out any lawful business unless there is a law authorizing a special class of corporations to carry out that business (Me. Rev. Stat. Ann. tit. 13-A, § 401(2)). If such a special class is authorized, no business corporation may carry on any business included in the special class. It follows that a business corporation may not render professional services that state law authorizes PCs to render. Business corporations may thus not provide physician services, through either shareholders or employees, since PCs may do so (Me. Rev. Stat. Ann. tit. 13, § 703(2)).

A business corporation may render psychological services in the state. This is implied by the psychology licensure law, which provides that, "[n]o industrial or business firm or corporation may sell or offer to the public or to other firms or corporations for remuneration any psychological services . . . unless such services are performed or supervised by individuals duly and appropriately licensed under this chapter as 'psychologist' " (Me. Rev. Stat. Ann. tit. 32, § 3813). The chairman of the Maine Board of Examiners of Psychologists confirmed that the board considers psychology business corporations permissible.[73]

Maine law does not permit multidisciplinary PCs. Persons licensed to render the same professional service may organize a PC "for the sole and specific purpose of rendering the same professional service" (Me. Rev. Stat. Ann. tit. 13, § 705). The statute specifies that osteopaths are deemed to render the same professional services as allopathic physicians and surgeons, but physicians and psychologists are not similarly mentioned. Thus, a PC with physician and psychologist shareholders is barred in Maine. The state's PC act does not specify whether persons licensed in a second profession may practice as employees of a PC that renders services in a different profession. According to Joe Wannamaker, counsel to the secretary of state's office, an employment relationship would probably also run afoul of the prohibition.[74]

### C. LLCs

Maine's limited liability company act took effect January 1, 1995. According to the act

[a] limited liability company may be organized . . . for any lawful purpose. If the purpose for which a limited liability company is orga-

nized or its form makes it subject to a special provision of law, the limited liability company shall also comply with that provision. This section is specifically intended to permit the formation of a professional limited liability company by a person or persons who may form a professional corporation under the Professional Service Corporation Act. The provisions of that Act are incorporated in this chapter by reference, with necessary changes being made. . . . (Me. Rev. Stat. Ann. tit. 31, § 611)

Since multidisciplinary PCs are not permitted, it appears that multidisciplinary LLCs are not either. The discussion above of employment of members of a second profession appears to apply to LLCs also.

## D. Networks

Maine's PPO regulations do not address the issue of multidisciplinary provider networks (Code Me. R. § 02-031-360 *et seq.*). Networks of physicians, psychologists, and allied health professionals may thus contract with third-party payers for the provision of services.

## MARYLAND

## A. Partnerships

A Maryland partnership may be formed to engage in business, including "every trade, occupation, or profession" (Md. Code Ann., Corps. & Assocs. § 9-101(b)). Neither the state's partnership laws nor the professional licensing laws prohibit licensees in different professions from practicing together. Psychologists, physicians, and allied health professionals may practice as partners and employees of a partnership, which may bill for their services.

Maryland's LLP act does not make specific reference to professional practice (Md. Code Ann., Corps. & Assocs. § 9-801 *et seq.*). The general partnership law, of which the LLP act is a part, states that nothing in its liability limitation provision limits the authority of professional licensure bodies (Md. Code Ann., Corps. & Assocs. § 9-307(d)). It thus appears that multidisciplinary professional practices are permitted on the same basis by LLPs as by general partnerships. Joe Stewart, counsel to the Department of Assessments and Taxation (which regulates corporations), indicated that this conclusion is correct.[75]

## B. Corporations

A Maryland business corporation may not employ physicians or psychologists to render professional services.  In a 1936 case the Maryland Court of Appeals held that a corporation that employed a registered optometrist was not engaged in the practice of optometry, contrasting the state's loose limitations on the corporate practice of optometry with its "stringent limitations" on the practice of law and medicine (*Dvorine v. Castleberg Jewelry Corp.*, 185 A. 562, Md. 1936). Although this case provides only weak support for prohibiting the corporate practice of medicine, stronger support is found in Maryland's PC act.  According to that statute, "a corporation that is eligible to be a professional corporation under this subtitle may not organize under any other corporate form permitted by this article" (Md. Code Ann., Corps. & Assocs § 5-102(2)).  The provision makes exceptions for four specific professions, but neither medicine nor psychology (which are eligible to form PCs) is among them (Md. Code Ann., Corps. & Assocs. §§ 5-101(g)(2), 5-102(3)).  Furthermore, the definition of "professional service," which expressly includes both medicine and psychology, describes such services as among those that "may not lawfully be rendered by a corporation under the Maryland General Corporation Law" (Md. Code Ann., Corps. & Assocs. § 5-101(g)(1)). Although a technical argument could be made against the application of these provisions, a more straightforward reading would likely prevail. Carolyn Wescott, counsel to Maryland's Board of Physician Quality Assurance, agrees that the corporate practice of medicine is barred.[76]  Employment by a business corporation thus appears to not be a viable form for joint practice in Maryland.

Under the Maryland PC act, as noted above, physicians and psychologists are each eligible to form PCs (Md. Code Ann., Corps. & Assocs. § 5-102(a)(2)).  PCs are limited to a single profession and may not engage in other activities (Md. Code Ann., Corps. & Assocs. §§ 5-102(a)(1), 5-104(a)).  However, a multiprofessional PC may be formed if the "combination of professional purposes is authorized by the licensing law of the State applicable to each profession in the combination" (Md. Code Ann., Corps. & Assocs. § 5-102(b)).  The combination of physicians and psychologists is not addressed in the respective practice acts, and Ms. Wescott indicated that none of the practice boards have promulgated either formal or informal rules on joint practices.[77]  She also indicated that the medical board has not been involved in enforcing the single-profession limitation as it has not yet given rise to any complaints.  It appears that the risks involved in forming a joint physician/psychologist PC in Maryland are probably low, but the permissibility of such arrangements is essentially an open question.

## C. LLCs

Maryland permits LLCs to be formed to render professional services, including medical and psychological services (Md. Code Ann., Corps. & Assocs. §§ 4A-101(p)(2), 4A-203(9)). In contrast to the state's PC act, the LLC law does not impose a single-profession limitation. This statutory silence suggests that physicians and psychologists may render their respective services as comembers or employees of an LLC. Mr. Stewart agreed that his agency shares this view.[78]

## D. Networks

Maryland's PPO act and other laws do not restrict provider networks (Md. Ann. Code art. 48A, § 655 *et seq.*). Psychologists, physicians, and allied health professionals may form and contract with networks in Maryland.

## MASSACHUSETTS

## A. Partnerships

There do not appear to be any statutory barriers to multidisciplinary partnerships in Massachusetts. Psychologists, physicians, and other health professionals may practice as partners and employees of a partnership. In fact, partnerships are explicitly permitted to employ psychologists (see Mass. Gen. Laws ch. 112, § 123(c)). A partnership may bill third-party payers for the professional services of its partners and employees.

There is no LLP statute in Massachusetts.

## B. Corporations

Business corporations in Massachusetts may employ and bill for the professional services of psychologists (see Mass. Gen. Laws ch. 112, § 123(c)). However, business corporations may not employ physicians.

Thus, the business corporation is not a viable vehicle for a multidisciplinary practice in Massachusetts.

In Massachusetts PCs must be formed for the purpose of rendering professional services and ancillary ones. PCs may render any form of professional service unless the licensing board for a particular profession prohibits its licensees from practicing in a multidisciplinary PC (see Mass. Gen. Laws ch. 156A, § 3). The authors are unaware of any such prohibition by a licensing board. Thus, a single PC may employ psychologists, psychiatrists and other physicians, and any combination of allied health professionals. A Massachusetts PC may have individually licensed professionals, partnerships (if all the partners are licensed professionals), and other PCs as shareholders (see Mass. Gen. Laws ch. 156A, § 10). A majority of the directors of every PC must be licensed professionals. All officers of a PC, other than its secretary, clerk, and treasurer, must be licensed professionals (see Mass. Gen. Laws ch. 156A, § 9). These relatively liberal provisions make the PC a very feasible structure for a multidisciplinary practice in Massachusetts.

### C. LLCs

To date, Massachusetts has not enacted an LLC statute. It is unclear how the state's courts and licensing boards would view a foreign LLC or PLLC that employed psychologists and physicians in Massachusetts.

### D. Networks

Psychologists, physicians, and allied health professionals may form and contract with networks in Massachusetts. In turn, a Massachusetts network may contract with insurance companies, Blue Cross/Blue Shield plans, and HMOs to have its affiliated practitioners be part or all of the payers' provider panels (see Mass. Gen. Laws ch. 176I, § 2).

## MICHIGAN

### A. Partnerships

There do not appear to be any statutory barriers to multidisciplinary partnerships of individual practitioners in Michigan. Psychologists, physicians (including psychiatrists), and allied health professionals may practice as partners and employees of a partnership. A partnership may bill third-party payers for the professional services of its partners and employees.

There is no LLP statute in Michigan.

## B. *Corporations*

Michigan's professional licensing statutes have been interpreted by courts and the Michigan attorney general to prohibit for-profit business corporations from practicing "learned professions" in the state. Both psychology and medicine are considered learned professions (see Op. Mich. Atty. Gen. No. 6592, July 10, 1989). Thus, for-profit business corporations may not employ psychologists and physicians.

In 1993 the Michigan attorney general rendered an opinion that allows nonprofit corporations to provide medical care through employed physicians (see Op. Mich. Atty. Gen. No. 6770). While the opinion did not mention psychologists, its reasoning fully supports employment of psychologists by nonprofit corporations. Thus, it appears that a Michigan nonprofit corporation is permitted to function as a multidisciplinary group practice, employing physicians, psychologists, and allied health professionals (such as social workers and professional counselors) and negotiating for their services with third-party payers.

Multidisciplinary PCs are not permissible in Michigan. The Michigan PC statute requires all the shareholders of a PC that employs health care professionals to have the same professional license (see Mich. Comp. Laws Ann. § 450.224(3)). In addition, a PC is prohibited from engaging in any business other than that of rendering the professional services for which it was specifically incorporated. Thus, a psychology PC may not employ physicians, and a medical PC may not employ psychologists. Moreover, a PC may not own shares in another PC unless the other PC practices only the same specific profession (see Mich. Comp. Laws Ann. § 450.227).

## C. LLCs

Standard LLCs in Michigan are explicitly prohibited from having as their purpose the practice of any profession (see Mich. Comp. Laws Ann. § 450.4201).

Michigan permits PLLCs, however. All members and managers of a PLLC that renders health care services must have the same professional license (see Mich. Comp. Laws Ann. § 450.4904(2)). In addition, a PLLC is prohibited from engaging in any business other than that of rendering the professional services for which it was specifically organized (see Mich. Comp. Laws Ann. § 450.4907(1)). Thus, a psychology PLLC may not employ physicians and a medical PLLC may not employ psychologists. Consequently, standard LLCs or PLLCs are not suitable vehicles for multidisciplinary practices in Michigan.

### D. Networks

Psychologists, physicians, and allied health professionals may form and contract with networks in Michigan. In turn, Michigan networks may contract with all types of third-party payers, including HMOs and insurance companies, to be all or part of their provider panels (see Mich. Comp. Laws Ann. §§ 333.21002, 550.57).

## MINNESOTA

### A. Partnerships

There do not appear to be any barriers to multidisciplinary partnerships under Minnesota partnership law. Psychologists, physicians (including psychiatrists), and allied health professionals may practice as partners and employees of a partnership. A partnership may bill third-party payers for the professional services of its partners and employees.

Minnesota recently enacted an LLP statute. The problems associated with forming a multidisciplinary LLP in Minnesota are addressed below.

### B. Corporations

There exists in Minnesota a general prohibition against professional services being practiced by a business corporation. The PC statute is the exception to this rule. A PC may be formed for either of two purposes. First, it may render one specific kind of professional service and "services ancillary thereto" (Minn. Stat. Ann. § 319A.04). Both medicine and psychology, however, are included in the law's list of professional services (Minn. Stat. Ann. § 319A.02(2)). It is not obvious that psychological services would be considered "ancillary" to the practice of medicine, or vice versa. Thus, a single PC could not practice both medicine and psychology under this provision.

The second possibility under the statute is that a PC be formed to render

> two or more kinds of professional services which are specifically authorized to be practiced in combination under the licensing laws of each of the professional services to be practiced. . . . (Minn. Stat. Ann. § 319A.04)

The state's licensing laws do not specifically authorize a joint medicine/psychology practice. The PC form thus does not appear to be available for a mixed group of practitioners in Minnesota.

A new amendment to the PC statute subjects LLPs and LLCs that provide professional services to the requirements of the PC statute (Minn. Stat. Ann. § 319A.02(7)). To the extent of any conflict between the LLP or LLC laws and the PC statute, the PC statute takes precedence" (Minn. Stat. Ann. § 319A.05). It thus appears that *all* corporations, LLPs, and LLCs that provide professional services are subject to the ban on unauthorized combinations of professional services. This leaves only the general partnership and network models for a mixed psychologist/physician entity in Minnesota.

## C. Limited Liability Companies

Minnesota law allows the formation of LLCs, but, for the reasons discussed above, an LLC may not employ both psychologists and physicians.

## D. Networks

Multispecialty networks are neither specifically authorized or barred by Minnesota statutory law. The law regulating HMOs, however, broadly permits an HMO to contract with "a group, professional corporation, or other organization" that provides the services of licensed health care professionals (Minn. Stat. Ann. § 62D.02(12)(3)). Preferred provider arrangements between a network and a licensed insurer also are permitted (Minn. Stat. Ann. §§ 62E.12-.13).

In 1993 the state gave specific authorization for the creation of fully integrated delivery systems (Minn. Stat. Ann. § 62N). The statute applies only to systems that provide the full range of health care services on a capitated basis; psychologists and physicians could be subcontractors of such networks.

## MISSISSIPPI

### A. *Partnerships*

A Mississippi partnership may be formed to engage in "every trade, occupation, or profession" (Miss. Code Ann. § 79-12-3). Neither the partnership laws nor the professional licensing laws impose any limitation on the ability of licensees in different professions to practice together. Psychologists, physicians, and allied health professionals may practice as partners and employees of a partnership, which may bill for their services.

Mississippi's LLP statute was enacted in 1995 and took effect July 1, 1995 (Miss. Code Ann. § 79-12-87 *et seq.*). The law does not impose any limits on the permissible purposes of an LLP or on who may hold partnership interests. However, Ray Bailey, staff attorney for the secretary of state, indicated that his office takes the position that the statute's failure to explicitly provide for the provision of professional services by LLPs means that such activity is barred.[79] Although this interpretation is open to question, it appears that an LLP is not a permissible vehicle for professional practice of any type in Mississippi at this time.

### B. *Corporations*

Mississippi's Board of Medical Licensure recently adopted a statement of "Corporate Practice of Medicine Policy." The statement lists a number of standards that must be observed—for example, that physicians have individual medical licenses, that their independence of medical judgment be maintained, that no kickbacks be paid, and that physicians retain discretion over fees. R. Doyle Bradshaw, executive officer of the board, and Stan Ingram, a private practitioner who serves as board counsel, confirmed that physicians may be employed by any entity, including a business corporation, as long as these standards are met.[80] Mr. Bradshaw and Mr. Ingram of the medical board, as well as Onetta Whitley, the assistant attorney general who advises the Board of Psychological Examiners, confirmed that there is no restriction on joint practices in the respective licensing laws.[81] A business corporation may employ both types of professionals for a joint mental health practice.

Under a 1995 reenactment of the Mississippi PC act, a PC may render professional services in two or more professions only "to the extent [that] the combination of professional purposes . . . is not prohibited by the licensing law of [the] state applicable to each profession in the combination" (1995 Miss. H.B. 937, § 5). Because, as was noted above, neither the medical nor the psychology practice acts or boards impose such a prohibition on joint medical/psychological practices, multidisciplinary mental health PCs are an option in Mississippi.

## C. LLCs

The same 1995 bill that reenacted the PC law also imposes comparable requirements on PLLCs (1995 Miss. H.B. 937, amending Miss. Code Ann. § 79-29-901 et seq.). If a particular combination of professions is not prohibited by the relevant licensing laws, the combination is permissible in a PLLC. In light of the absence of such prohibitions under Mississippi law, it appears that a PLLC may practice both medicine and psychology in the state.

## D. Networks

Mississippi's 1995 PPO law does not impose any limitations on the membership of provider panels (1995 Miss. S.B. 2669). Psychologists, physicians, and allied health professionals may form networks and contract with third-party payers to provide services.

# MISSOURI

## A. Partnerships

A Missouri partnership may be formed to engage in "every trade, occupation, or profession" (Mo. Rev. Stat. § 358.020(2)). Neither the partnership laws nor the professional licensing laws impose any limitations on the ability of licensees in different professions to practice together. Psychologists, physicians, and allied health professionals may practice as partners and employees of a partnership, which may bill for their services.

Missouri's 1995 LLP act imposes no limitations on the permissible purposes of an LLP (Mo. Rev. Stat. § 358.440 et seq.). Different types of mental health professionals may practice jointly as partners or employees of an LLP. Penney Rector and Evan Buchheim, the assistant attorneys general who advise the Missouri State Committee of Psychologists and Board of Registration for the Healing Arts, respectively, agreed with this conclusion.[82]

## B. *Corporations*

Missouri business corporations may be organized for any lawful purposes unless "required to be organized exclusively under other provisions of [the] law"; the state's PC act, however, imposes no such explicit requirement (Mo. Rev. Stat. §§ 351.020, 356.011 *et seq.*). A 1979 opinion by the Missouri attorney general, however, suggests that the prohibition on the corporate practice of professions remains vital in the state (Mo. AG Lexis 27, July 31). The question presented involved employment of a dentist by a corporation. Although acknowledging that the state's business corporation act permits incorporation for any lawful purpose, the attorney general concluded that, since business corporations may not be licensed as dentists, the practice of dentistry would not be a lawful purpose. Although the attorney general was not addressing medical practices, the underlying statutory provisions are similar, and the opinion's reasoning would appear to have equal force with respect to physicians.

Missouri's PC act permits PCs to be formed to render certain types of professional services, including medicine and psychology, each of which is one "type" (Mo. Rev. Stat. § 356.021(5)(b)). PCs may render "one or more types of professional service . . . to the extent that such combination of professional services . . . is expressly permitted by the licensing authorities that regulate each of such professions" (Mo. Rev. Stat. § 356.051). Ms. Rector and Mr. Buchheim indicated that the relevant professional boards have never taken formal positions on joint physician–psychologist PCs, but that the boards would not oppose them.[83]

## C. LLCs

Under Missouri law an LLC may "conduct or promote any lawful businesses or purposes within [the] state or any other jurisdiction" (Mo. Rev. Stat. § 347.035). "Business" is defined to include "every trade, occupation or profession" (Mo. Rev. Stat. § 347.015(4)). Inasmuch as the medical and psychology practice acts do not prohibit joint practice by those professionals, as Ms. Rector and Mr. Buchheim agreed, they may carry on a multidisciplinary practice as comembers or employees of an LLC.[84]

## D. Networks

Missouri does not regulate provider networks. Psychologists, physicians, and allied health professionals may form networks and contract with third-party payers to provide services.

## MONTANA

### A. Partnerships

A Montana partnership may engage in "every trade, occupation, or profession" (Mont. Code Ann. § 35-10-102(1)). Furthermore, the medical practice act's prohibition on the payment or receipt of payment for services not actually rendered is accompanied by a disclaimer that "[t]his prohibition does not preclude the legal functioning of lawful professional partnerships, corporations, or associations" (Mont. Code Ann. § 37-3-322(5)). The implication is that physicians may form professional partnerships.

Nevertheless, the Board of Medical Examiners' apparent interpretation of "unprofessional conduct" by physicians may impose some limits on the formation and operation of multidisciplinary partnerships that include physicians. Under rules of the Board (which until 1995 had been part of the state's statutory medical pratice act), "unprofessional conduct" is defined to include:

> Except as provided in this subsection, practicing medicine as the partner, agent or employee of, or in joint venture with, a person who does not hold a license to practice medicine within the state; however, this does not prohibit:
>
> (a) the incorporation of an individual licensee or group of licensees as a professional service corporation under Title 35, chapter 4, MCA;
>
> (b) a single consultation with or a single treatment by a person licensed to practice medicine and surgery in another state or territory of the United States or foreign country;
>
> (c) the organization of a professional limited liability company under Title 35, chapter 8, MCA, for the providing of professional services as defined in Title 35, chapter 8, MCA;
>
> (d) practicing medicine as the partner, agent or employee of or in joint venture

with a hospital, medical assistance facility, or other licensed health care provider; however:

(i) the partnership, agency, employment, or joint venture must be evidenced by a written agreement containing language to the effect that the relationship created by the agreement may not affect the exercise of the physician's independent judgment in the practice of medicine; and

(ii) the physician's independent judgment in the practice of medicine must in fact be unaffected by the relationship; and

(iii) the physician may not be required to refer any patient to a particular provider or supplier or take any other action the physician determines not to be in the patient's best interest[.] Mont. Admin. R. 8.28.423(20).

A physician may thus enter into a partnership with any "other licensed health care provider" if the partnership is structured to comply with the three provisos in subsection d, which are intended to preserve physicians' independent judgment. Ms. England confirmed that the Board of Medical Examiners has interpreted the term "other licensed health care provider" as including psychologists.[85]  A properly structured joint physician–psychologist partnership is therefore permitted.

Ms. England confirmed that the Board of Medical Examiners has interpreted, and will continue to interpret, the term "other licensed health care provider" as including psychologists. A properly structured joint physician-psychologist partnership would therefore be permitted.

Montana's LLP act, enacted in 1995, does not limit the permissible purposes of an LLP, and it indicates that the law's definition of a partnership includes LLPs for "all licensing laws, whether for professionals or otherwise," implying that LLPs may be formed for professional practice (Mont. Code Ann. § 35-10-102(5)(B)). Since the medical practice rule discussed above applies to "partners," the analysis above appears to apply to LLPs as well as to general partnerships, and LLPs would be permitted under the circumstances described there.

## B. Corporations

In general, Montana business corporations may be organized to carry on any lawful business (Mont. code Ann. § 35-4-205). However, a business corporation, unlike a PC, is not among the listed exceptions to the physician employment prohibition in the medical practice rules (Mont. Admin. R. 8.28.423(20), quoted above). Because the board's regulation precludes employment of physicians by a business corporation, such a corporation may not serve as a vehicle for a multidisciplinary mental health practice. Ms. England confirmed that the board holds this position.[86]

In contrast, an express exception to the provision quoted permits physicians to practice in PCs (Mont. Admin. R. 8.28.423(20)(a)).

As to whether a multidisciplinary PC is permitted, a PC may be organized

> [o]nly for the purpose of rendering professional services and services ancillary thereto within a single profession, except that a professional corporation may be incorporated for the purpose of rendering professional services within two or more professions and for any purpose or purposes for which corporations may be organized under the Montana Business Corporation Act to the extent that such combination of professional purposes or professional and business purposes is permitted by the licensing laws and rules of [the] state applicable to such professions. (Mont. Code Ann. § 35-4-205)

Inasmuch as the practice boards agree that the physician-psychologist combination is permitted under their respective statutes and rules, as Ms. England of the Board of Medical Examiners and Cheryl Brandt of the Board of Psychology confirmed, members of the two professions may practice together as coowners or employees of a Montana PC.[87]

## C. LLCs

Montana has a PLLC law that mirrors its PC Act, permitting PLLCs with more than one type of professional if the relevant licensing laws and rules so permit (Mont. Code Ann. § 35-8-1301). The Board of Medical Examiners' rule on "unprofessional conduct," quoted above, also makes an express exception for PLLCs, mirroring the one for PCs (Mont. Admin. R. 8.28.423(20)(c)). Physicians may therefore be PLLC members if the provisos discussed above are observed. As the personnel at the professional boards agreed, the licensing laws and rules permit the medical/psychological combination of professions, and the PLLC form is a viable option for joint mental health practice.[88]

## D. Networks

Montana's PPO statute is limited to workers' compensation PPOs, and it does not limit panel membership (Mont. Code Ann. § 39-71-1107).

Psychologists, physicians, and allied health professionals may form networks and contract with third-party payers to provide services.

## NEBRASKA

### A. *Partnerships*

The Nebraska partnership statute imposes no limitations on the permissible purposes of a general partnership (Neb. Rev. Stat. § 67-101 *et seq.*). Neither the partnership laws nor the professional licensing laws impose any limitations on the ability of licensees in different professions to practice together. Psychologists, physicians, and allied health professionals may practice as partners and employees of a partnership, which may bill for their services.

Nebraska does not have an LLP statute.

### B. *Corporations*

Corporations may not be organized under Nebraska's business corporation act "to perform any of [the] personal services specified" in the definitional section of the state's PC act (Neb. Rev. Stat. § 21-2003). Because the definition of professional services includes services rendered by a physician or surgeon, business corporations are precluded from employing physicians (Neb. Rev. Stat. § 21-2202(1)). As a result, despite the fact that psychological services are not expressly listed, a business corporation would not be a permissible form for a joint physician/psychologist practice.

Under Nebraska law, a PC may render only one type of professional service and may not engage in any other profession (Neb. Rev. Stat. § 21-2205). However, the definition of "professional service" provides that [f]or purposes of the act, those professions pertaining to the diagnosis, care, and treatment of humans shall be considered to be of the same profession" (Neb. Rev. Stat. § 21-2202(1)). Although psychological services are not specifically listed as being a professional service, as is medicine, the definition states that the list is not exhaustive. Greg Lemon, an attorney who serves as deputy secretary of state, agreed that medicine and psychology "pertain to the diagnosis, care, and treatment of humans."[89] Personnel at the practice boards agreed that there are no limitations on multidisciplinary practices.[90] It thus appears that physicians and psychologists may practice together as shareholders in a Nebraska PC.

## C. LLCs

According to Nebraska's LLC statute, an LLC may render professional services (Neb. Rev. Stat. § 21-2603(15)); however, the LLC is required to file a registration certificate issued to it by "the regulatory body of the particular profession for which [it] is licensed to do business" and to certify the licensure of all members, managers, and professional employees to perform "the professional services for which [it] is organized" (Neb. Rev. Stat. § 21-2631). The first clause quoted implies that LLCs are limited to the practice of a single profession. However, Mr. Lemon indicated that the secretary of state's office interprets LLCs to be available to professionals under the same circumstances as PCs, notwithstanding the LLC act's different language.[91] Since joint physician/psychologist PCs are permitted, he concluded that LLCs combining the same professions would not be challenged. Given that the practice boards also do not object to joint practices, LLCs appear to be a viable option under Nebraska law and enforcement policy.

## D. Networks

Nebraska does not regulate provider networks. Psychologists, physicians, and allied health professionals may form networks and contract with third-party payers to provide services.

## NEVADA

### A. Partnerships and Professional Associations

A Nevada partnership may be formed to engage in "every trade, occupation or profession" (Nev. Rev. Stat. § 87.020(2)). Neither the partnership laws nor the professional licensing laws impose any limitations on the ability of licensees in different professions to practice together. Psychologists, physicians, and allied health professionals may practice as partners and employees of a partnership, which may bill for their services.

Nevada adopted an LLP statute in 1995 (S.B. 347). The law permits general partnerships to convert to LLPs by filing with the secretary of state a "brief statement of the professional service rendered by the partnership." This makes it clear that the LLP may render at least one professional service, but, like the remainder of the law, neither bars nor explicitly permits multidisciplinary LLPs. Kateri Cavin, the deputy attorney general who advises the secretary of state, agreed that this remains a gray area under the new law.[92]  Therefore, it is not clear whether LLPs are an option for joint physician/psychologist practice under Nevada law.

Nevada law also provides for "professional associations" (PAs), which are not subject to the state partnership law (Nev. Rev. Stat. § 89.200). The PA statute, however, explicitly limits PA membership to persons licensed to render "the same specific professional services" for which the PA was organized (Nev. Rev. Stat. § 89.230).  The statute does not expressly limit the PA's permissible activity (as distinct from its membership) to the single profession, suggesting that licensees in a second profession could practice as employees of the PA.  Ms. Cavin indicated that such employment would probably not be challenged but confirmed that ownership of a PA by members of multiple professions, such as physicians and psychologists, is not permissible.[93]

## B. Corporations

In a 1977 opinion the Nevada attorney general addressed the employment of physicians by business corporations (Nev. AG Lexis 19, October 3).  Relying on cases from other jurisdictions as well as the legislative creation of the PC entity for the provision of professional services, the attorney general opined that "no corporation organized under the General Corporation Law of Nevada . . . may lawfully engage in the practice of medicine. . . . "  However, Larry Leslie, counsel to Nevada's Board of Medical Examiners, indicated that the board does not enforce the prohibition because it is not expressly imposed by the medical practice act, and Ms. Cavin stated that the attorney general would not be involved in enforcement.[94]  It thus appears that the risk posed by a business corporation's employment of physicians is low, making such an arrangement a potentially viable one for a joint mental health practice.

With certain exceptions, a Nevada PC may be organized "only for the purpose of rendering one specific type of professional service and may not engage in any business other than rendering the professional service for which it was organized and services reasonably related thereto . . . " (Nev. Rev. Stat. § 89.050(1)).  An exception exists for medical and osteopathic physicians to practice in a single PC, but no exception exists for physicians and psychologists (Nev. Rev. Stat. § 89.050(2)(b)).  The only argument for permitting a multidisciplinary mental health practice, then, is that psychological services are "services reasonably related" to medical services, or vice versa.  However, Ms. Cavin of the attorney general's office explained that the test for whether services are "reasonably related" is whether they are licensed by the same professional board.[95] Since psychologists and physicians are licensed by distinct boards, she indicated that members of both professions may not practice as coowners or employees of the same PC.

## C. LLCs

According to Nevada law, an LLC may be organized for any lawful purpose except banking or insurance (Nev. Rev. Stat. § 86.141). This suggests that the LLC form is available for professional practices of all types. However, the same 1995 legislation that created LLPs also provided for PLLCs to practice accounting, without reference to other professions. Ms. Cavin indicated that filings of LLCs in single professions other than accounting will continue to be accepted. As to multidisciplinary LLCs, she replied that the issue had not arisen and that no policy is yet in place.[96] The practice boards indicated that they have not considered the issue but doubt they would raise any objection.[97] Although there is no express statutory prohibition, it remains uncertain whether LLCs may carry on joint physician/psychologist practices in Nevada.

## D. Networks

Nevada does not regulate provider networks. Psychologists, physicians, and allied health professionals may form networks and contract with third-party payers to provide services.

## NEW HAMPSHIRE

### A. Partnerships

A New Hampshire partnership may be formed to engage in "every trade, occupation, or profession" (N.H. Rev. Stat. Ann. § 304-A:2(II)). Neither the partnership laws nor the professional licensing laws impose any limitations on the ability of licensees in different professions to practice together. Psychologists, physicians, and allied health professionals may practice as partners and employees of a partnership, which may bill for their services.

New Hampshire does not have an LLP law.

## B. *Corporations*

New Hampshire has no statutes or case law addressing the corporate practice of medicine. Its PC act implicitly addresses the question, however, in that its definition of "professional service" refers to services "that may not lawfully be rendered by a corporation organized under the law of [the] state applicable to business corporations" (N.H. Rev. Stat. Ann. § 294-A(1)(VI)). Both medicine and psychology are listed as professional services. However, Assistant Attorney General Doug Jones, who advises the registration boards for medicine and psychology, indicated that the practice boards have never been compelled to address the corporate practice question.[98] Given the prevalence of corporate employment of both psychologists and physicians (e.g., by hospitals and HMOs), he doubts that the boards would challenge corporate employment unless it posed a risk of compromising the independent judgment of the professionals involved. Although the law is not clear, it appears as a practical matter that in New Hampshire a business corporation may employ both physicians and psychologists to render services.

Both medicine and psychology are among the professional services in which a New Hampshire PC may engage (N.H. Rev. Stat. Ann. § 294-A:1(VI)). PCs are limited to a single profession unless the particular combination "is permitted by the licensing laws of [the] state applicable to such professions and rules under those laws" (N.H. Rev. Stat. Ann. § 294-A:2). The physician and psychologist licensing laws and regulations, however, do not address any particular combinations. Mr. Jones indicated that the relevant practice boards have never had occasion to opine on whether a physician/psychologist combination is permissible.[99] Although noting that the boards normally challenge business arrangements only if they present a risk of substandard professional practice, he was not willing to say that a multidisciplinary practice would be permitted unless it raised such issues. The lack of enforcement activity in this area suggests that a joint physician/psychologist PC is unlikely to be challenged, but it must be noted that the legality of such an arrangement remains uncertain.

## C. LLCs

The provisions of New Hampshire's professional LLC act relevant to multidisciplinary practices are identical to those of the PC act, discussed above (N.H. Rev. Stat. Ann. § 304-D:2). For the reasons discussed there, the permissibility of an LLC with both physicians and psychologists is similarly uncertain.

## D. Networks

New Hampshire's PPO statute and other laws do not restrict provider networks (N.H. Rev. Stat. Ann. § 420-C:1 *et seq.*) Psychologists, physicians, and allied health professionals may form and contract with networks in New Hampshire.

## NEW JERSEY

### A. Partnerships

The regulations of the New Jersey Boards of Psychology and Medical Examiners allow psychologists and physicians to practice in multidisciplinary general partnerships with practitioners in closely allied health care professions so long as each practitioner retains professional autonomy. Psychology, medicine, social work, and nursing, among other professions, are specifically identified as being closely allied health care professions(see N.J.A.C. §§ 13:42-7.2(b)), 13:35-6.16(f)(2). However, a partnership that employs one or more physicians must have at least one physician partner, so that all physician employees are supervised by another physician (see N.J.A.C. § 13:35-6.16(f)(3)(i)). The partnership may bill third-party payers for the professional services of its partners and employees.

There is no LLP statute in New Jersey.

### B. Corporations

A multidisciplinary practice may not be organized as a business corporation because such a corporation may not employ either psychologists or physicians except in very limited settings (e.g., to treat its own employees; see N.J.A.C. §§ 13:42-7.5, 13:35-6.16(f)(4)).

Multidisciplinary PCs are permitted in New Jersey. They may have shareholders and employees who are practitioners in closely allied health care professions so long as each practitioner retains professional autonomy. As discussed above, the New Jersey Board of Medical Examiners has clarified that psychology, medicine, social work, and nursing, among other professions, are closely allied health care professions (see N.J.S.A. § 14A:17-

3(3), N.J.A.C. § 13:35-6.16(f)(2)). Psychologists may hold a majority of shares, directorships, and offices in a multidisciplinary PC. There are no requirements regarding which license must be held by the officers or directors of a PC (see N.J.S.A. § 14A:17-6). However, a PC that employs one or more physicians must have at least one physician officer, so that all physician employees are supervised by another physician (See N.J.A.C. § 13:35-6.16(f)(3)(i)).

## C. LLCs

New Jersey enacted an LLC statute in 1993 (see N.J.S.A. § 42:2B-1–70). The law does not provide specifically for professional LLCs, however. The New Jersey attorney general has opined that the form is a permissible one for professionals, but that the relevant licensing boards may prohibit professional LLCs.[100] The regulations governing the practice of medicine list certain "acceptable professional practice forms," but do not address the LLC form (N.J.A.C. § 13:35-6.16(f)). A deputy attorney general who advises the Board of Medical Examiners indicated that the LLC form is thus unavailable to physicians.[101] At present, the LLC form is thus unavailable for joint practices that include physicians.

## D. Networks

Psychologists and physicians are permitted to form and to enter into contracts with networks in New Jersey so long as they retain their professional autonomy (see N.J.A.C. §§ 13:42-7.6, 13:35-6.16(h)). A psychologist must disclose his or her financial arrangements (including cost containment incentives) with a network to patients whose health care benefits are arranged by the network.

## NEW MEXICO

## A. Partnerships

There do not appear to be any barriers to multidisciplinary partnerships in New Mexico. Psychologists, physicians, and allied health professionals may practice as partners and employees of a partnership.

New Mexico law provides for LLPs, and imposes no limitations on their permissible purposes. N.M. Stat. Ann. § 54-1-44 *et seq.* Inasmuch as the professional licensing laws do not prohibit joint medical–psychological practice arrangements, it appears that the LLP form may be used for this purpose.

## B. Corporations

A 1987 opinion by the New Mexico attorney general squarely endorsed the employment of physicians by business corporations (Op. Atty. Gen. 39, N.M. A.G. Lexis 45, July 30). As long as the corporation does not "engage in conduct amounting to the practice of medicine by exerting lay control of professional medical judgments," physicians may practice as corporate employees. The attorney general relied on the fact that, while dentists and podiatrists are expressly barred from corporate practice, the state's medical practice act has no express prohibition. The state's psychology practice act also lacks such a prohibition, suggesting that a business corporation also may have psychologists as members or employees. The business corporation act imposes no limitations on permissible business purposes, and staffers from the medicine and psychology licensing boards indicated that they see no basis for challenging multidisciplinary practice arrangements.[102] It therefore appears that the multidisciplinary business corporation is a viable option in New Mexico as long as the corporation does not control the professional judgment of the physicians and psychologists.

A New Mexico PC, however, may render "only one specific type of professional service and services ancillary thereto and shall not engage in any business other than rendering the professional service which it was organized to render" (N.M. Stat. Ann. § 53-6-5). This provision forecloses the option of having members of a second profession practice as either coowners or employees of a PC. The New Mexico Corporation Commission takes the same view of the law, according to Manuel Salinas, head of the Corporations Division of the commission.[103]

## C. LLCs

Under New Mexico's LLC act,

[a] limited liability company may conduct or promote any lawful business or purpose. If the purpose for which a limited liability company is organized makes it subject to provisions of other laws, the limited

liability company shall also be subject to such provisions.  (N.M. Stat. Ann. § 53-19-6)

The act makes no mention of the provision of professional services by LLCs.  It thus appears that the practice of professions by LLCs is permitted.  Since the licensing laws of the medical and psychological professions do not bar multidisciplinary practice arrangements, it appears that LLCs are a viable vehicle for joint practices.  Mr. Salinas of the Corporation Commission indicated that his agency would consider such an LLC permissible under the statute.[104]

## D. Networks

The state's 1993 preferred provider arrangements law does not restrict provider networks (N.M. Stat. Ann. § 59A-22A-1 *et seq.*).  Psychologists, physicians, and allied health professionals may form and contract with networks in New Mexico.

## NEW YORK

### A. Partnerships

Multidisciplinary partnerships of psychologists and physicians are not permitted in New York.  A recent amendment to the state's partnership law requires that all partners of a professional partnership that provides medical services be physicians.  While psychologists may form professional partnerships with other professionals, such as allied health professionals, the partnership form of organization is not available for a joint medical/ psychological practice.

The partnership statute authorizes the creation of professional LLPs, which are called "registered limited liability partnerships" (RLLPs).  As with general partnerships, however, all partners in a medical services RLLP must be licensed physicians (N.Y. Partnership Law § 121-1500(q)).  Thus, the RLLP is not an option for physicians seeking to conduct a joint practice with any other professionals, including psychologists.  Psychologists, however, are not subject to a comparable single-profession limitation.  They may therefore form RLLPs with other types of allied mental health professionals as long as the other professionals are also not subject to a single-profession limitation.  Dr. Kathleen Doyle, executive secretary of the Board of Psychology, a division of the state's Department of Education (which licenses professionals), confirmed these conclusions as follows:

> [A] psychologist and a certified social worker could form a professional service limited liability company or registered limited liability partnership for the purpose of practicing the professions of psychology and certified social work. A physician and a psychologist could *not* form such a company or partnership.[105]

## B. Corporations

New York courts and the New York Department of Health have issued opinions that interpret New York professional licensing statutes in a manner that creates a very stringent version of the corporate practice of medicine doctrine. Unless a business corporation is licensed as a health care provider (e.g., a hospital) or an HMO, it may not employ licensed health care practitioners or bill third-party payers for the professional services of such practitioners (see also discussion below under "Networks").

In New York PCs are tightly regulated. A PC may be formed only for the practice of a single health profession, such as psychology, medicine, or nursing. It may have as shareholders, directors, and officers only individuals who are licensed in that single profession in New York and who are or have been engaged in the practice of that profession in that PC (N.Y. Bus. Corp. Law §§ 1507-1508). A single PC may not employ both psychologists and physicians (N.Y. Bus. Corp. Law § 1503(a)). Multidisciplinary PCs are clearly not permitted in New York.

## C. LLCs

In New York a standard LLC (i.e., an LLC other than a PLLC) may not be formed to do "any business for which another statute specifically requires some other business entity or natural person to be formed or used for such business" (N.Y. Limited Liability Co. Law § 201, as added by S. 7511-A § 1, 1994). As Dr. Doyle confirmed in her letter cited earlier, standard LLCs may not be used for professional practices.

The New York LLC statute also provides for PLLCs, which may render only professional services that one or more PLLC members are authorized to practice (LLC law § 1206). The same analysis given for RLLPs applies to PLLCs: in PLLCs that practice medicine, all members must be licensed physicians, precluding joint medicine/psychology PLLCs (LLC Law § 1207(b)). Again, however, nothing in the law precludes psychologists from entering into PLLCs with other allied health professionals. Dr. Doyle's letter applies to PLLCs as well as RLLPs and confirms that psychologists may join such arrangements.

### D. Networks

In New York a network may be formed for one purpose only: to contract *with a single HMO* for the services of practitioners who have entered into agreements with the network. Such entities must be licensed by the state as IPAs. A licensed IPA may have both physicians and psychologists as members. The IPA must maintain financial records that account for all funds received from the HMO and for disbursements of those funds (see 10 N.Y.C.R.R. §§ 98.2(aa), 98.4(c), 98.5(b)(6)(iv), 98.18). Legislation that would allow IPAs to contract with multiple HMOs in the state has repeatedly been proposed but never enacted.

Two opinions issued in 1991 by the New York Department of Health indicate that the only entities that may act as a network in New York are licensed IPAs. Significantly, both opinions involved networks that wanted to coordinate the provision of behavioral health care services by independent practitioners. [106] As noted above, licensed IPAs are permitted to contract only with a single HMO. It follows that when any New York payer other than an HMO wants to establish a limited panel of preferred practitioners, it must contract *directly* with the providers, rather than doing so through a network. Despite the categorical position of the New York Department of Health in these letters, there are numerous networks operating in the state that are not licensed IPAs and thus are not in compliance with the department's interpretation of New York law. Although it appears that state regulators have not moved to challenge these arrangements, mental health professionals should note that they are not free of legal risk.

## NORTH CAROLINA

### A. Partnerships

A North Carolina partnership may be formed to engage in any business, including "every trade, occupation, or profession" (N.C. Gen. Stat. § 59-32(2)). Neither the partnership laws or the professional licensing laws prohibit licensees in different professions from practicing together. Psychologists, physicians, and allied health professionals may therefore practice as partners and employees of a partnership, which may bill for their services.

The state LLP law does not mention the practice of professions (N.C. Gen. Stat. § 59-84.2 *et seq.*). It thus appears that physicians and psychologists may practice as LLP partners or employees on the same basis as in a general partnership. John Collar, Director of the Corporations Division, agreed with this conclusion.[107]

## B. *Corporations*

In a 1955 opinion the North Carolina attorney general concluded that a business corporation could not employ physicians (Op. N.C. Atty. Gen., December 9). However, Jim Wilson, an attorney for the Board of Medical Examiners, indicated that the prohibition is no longer enforced.[108] He noted that the state's medical practice act does not contain an express prohibition on the practice of medicine by a business corporation, as, for example, the legal licensure law does for attorneys (N.C. Gen. Stat. § 84-5). Unless the corporate employment affected a physician's exercise of professional judgment, according to Mr. Wilson, the board would not take an interest in it. It can be concluded, therefore, that employment of physicians and psychologists by a business corporation, while not risk free, is unlikely to be challenged.

In North Carolina PCs are generally limited to a single profession and may not engage in any other business (N.C. Gen. Stat. § 55B-14). There are two exceptions, however, of particular significance in the mental health area:

A professional corporation may also be formed by and between or among:

(1) A licensed psychologist and a physician practicing psychiatry to render psychotherapeutic and related services . . .

(4) A physician practicing psychiatry, or a licensed psychologist, or

both, and a certified clinical specialist in psychiatric and mental health nursing, or a certified clinical social worker, or both, to render psychotherapeutic and related services that the respective stockholders are licensed, certified, or otherwise approved to provide . . .

Although the law does not define "psychotherapeutic and related services," personnel at the practice boards explained that they consider the term to encompass all activities within the professionals' respective scopes of practice.[109] As long as a PC does not provide unrelated medical services (e.g., orthopedics, obstetrics/gynecology) in conjunction with psychology services, psychiatrists and psychologists may practice together, as either coshareholders or employees, in a North Carolina PC. Both types of professionals also may practice with the other allied mental health professionals specified in the PC statute.

### C. LLCs

North Carolina LLCs are permitted to render professional services "only to the extent that, and subject to the conditions and limitations under which, a professional corporation may engage in rendering professional services under [the PC act] and under the applicable licensing statute" (N.C. Gen. Stat. § 57C-2-01(c)). As noted above, the PC act specifically authorizes certain combinations of mental health professionals (N.C. Gen. Stat. § 55B-14). Since the medical or psychological practice acts also do not impede multidisciplinary practices, it appears that joint psychiatrist/psychologist LLCs for the rendering of psychotherapeutic and related services are an option in North Carolina.

### D. Networks

Provider networks are not restricted under North Carolina law, including its PPO statute (N.C. Gen. Stat. § 58-50-55). Psychologists, physicians, and allied health professionals may form and contract with networks.

# NORTH DAKOTA

## A. Partnerships

A North Dakota partnership may be formed to engage in "every trade, occupation, or profession" (N.D. Cent. Code § 45-13-01(1); current § 45-05-01 is identical). Neither the partnership laws nor the professional licensing laws impose any limitations on the ability of licensees in different professions to practice together. Psychologists, physicians, and allied health professionals may practice as partners and employees of a partnership, which may bill for their services.

In 1995 North Dakota enacted a law providing for LLPs (N.D. Cent. Code § 45-22-01). A separate statute regulates all "professional organizations," which are defined to include PLLPs as well as PCs and PLLCs (N.D. Cent. Code § 10-31-01). A 1995 amendment to the law specifies that a PLLP may issue partnership interests "only to individuals who are licensed to render the same specific professional service as those for which the partnership was registered" (N.D. Cent. Code § 10-31-07.3). However, the amendment also permits creation of professional organizations to render two or more kinds of professional services "specifically authorized to be practiced in combination under the licensing laws of each of the professional services" (N.D. Cent. Code § 10-31-04(1)). The licensing laws are silent on this point, however, and the relevant practice boards have never decided whether the physician/psychologist combination is permitted, according to Rolf Sletten, executive secretary of the Board of Medical Examiners, and Dr. Chris Kuchler, president of the Board of Psychology Examiners.[110] Although neither thought it likely that such an arrangement would be challenged, both emphasized that the question is unanswered at this point.

## B. Corporations

Business corporations, in contrast to PLLPs, PCs, and PLLCs, are not subject to the professional organizations law discussed above (N.D. Cent. Code § 10-31-01(7)). North Dakota's business corporation law permits incorporation for any business purpose(s), unless another state statute requires incorporation for any of those purposes under a different law (N.D. Cent. Code § 10-19.1-08). Statutory law does not otherwise address employment of physicians by business corporations, except specifically to permit *hospitals* to employ physicians "[n]otwithstanding any other provision of law" (N.D. Cent. Code § 43-17-42). As long as the employment relationship does not actually affect the physician's independent medical judgment, and the employment contract contains language protecting that judgment, the hospital may employ the physician and "may not be deemed to be engaged in the practice of medicine."

As to employment by business corporations other than hospitals, Mr. Sletten indicated that the medical board relies on a 1990 letter written by the state attorney general, even though the letter is not a formal opinion.[111] After reviewing cases (including one from North Dakota prohibiting the corporate practice of architecture), the attorney general opined that a business corporation could not employ physicians to provide medical care.[112]

Despite the informal nonbinding nature of the letter, Mr. Sletten noted that the board considers it the governing rule at this time. Because of this prohibition, employment by a business corporation is not a permissible approach to multidisciplinary practice in North Dakota.

A North Dakota PC may have as shareholders only individuals licensed to render the "same professional service" as the PC (N.D. Cent. Code § 10-31-01(5)). However, the new provision of the professional organization law, discussed above, appears to modify the preexisting single-profession requirement. The 1995 amendment, authorizing multidisciplinary practices if permitted under the professional licensure laws, applies to PCs as well (N.D. Cent. Code §§ 10-31-01(7), 10-31-04(1)). As noted above, however, it is unclear whether the licensing laws permit joint physician/psychologist practices, so the availability of PCs for such a purpose is uncertain.

### C. LLCs

Although North Dakota's PLLC law requires that members be licensed to render the same professional service, PLLCs are also subject to the professional organization statute discussed above, which relaxed the single-profession limitation (N.D. Cent. Code §§ 10-31-01(7), 10-31-04(1)). For the reasons discussed above, it cannot be said with certainty whether physicians and psychologists may jointly practice in a PLLC.

### D. Networks

North Dakota's PPO statute does not impose any limitations on the ability of different professionals to practice jointly (N.D. Cent. Code § 26.1-47-01). Psychologists, physicians, and allied health professionals may form networks and contract with third-party payers to provide services.

## OHIO

### A. Partnerships

The Ohio code provides broadly that partnerships may be formed to engage in a business, which is defined as "every trade, occupation, or profession" (Ohio Rev. Code Ann. § 1775.01). Nothing in the partnership act restricts the practice of multiple professions by a partnership. Moreover, the Board of Psychology stated that it would not be concerned about physicians and psychologists practicing together in a partnership and noted that several such arrangements already exist in Ohio.[113] The Medical Board, however, is concerned that such arrangements could constitute fee splitting under the medical practice act (Ohio Rev. Code Ann. § 4731.22).[114] The Medical Board has received a significant number of inquiries about such multidisciplinary arrangements but has not yet taken a position on their permissibility. The board suggests that written requests for opinions be submitted before forming any such entities, although a response could take as long as several months.

Effective July 1, 1994, partnerships may register as partnerships having limited liability (PLL) (Ohio Rev. Code Ann. § 1775.61). There are no restrictions against physicians and psychologists organizing and registering as a PLL. Katie Phipps, an attorney in the secretary of state's office, confirmed this interpretation.[115] Again, however, the Ohio medical board is concerned that such arrangements could result in impermissible fee splitting.

### B. Corporations

Historically, Ohio's medical practice and business corporations acts have been interpreted to prohibit the corporate practice of medicine. The medical practice act provides that (1) only licensed persons may practice medicine (implying that corporations, which cannot be licensed, may not practice medicine) and (2) physicians may not split fees with any other person(s) (such as a corporation or its shareholders) (Ohio Rev. Code Ann. §§ 4731.41, 4731.22(B)(17)). The corporations act originally provided that a business corporation could be formed for any purpose(s) other than carrying on the practice of any profession. The act was subsequently amended to provide that designated classes of corporations could be incorporated as provided elsewhere in the code (e.g., under the professional association act, § 1701.03; see generally Op. Ohio Atty. Gen. No. 52-1751, 1952) (a corporation that charges and collects a fee from patients for medical treatment performed by licensed physicians as employees of such corporation is unlawfully engaged in the practice of medicine).

Effective July 7, 1994, however, Senate Bill No. 74 further amended the corporations act to provide that a general business corporation "may be formed . . . for the purpose of carrying on the practice of any profession" (Ohio Rev. Code Ann. § 1701.3(B)). This amended section would therefore appear to undermine one of the significant statutory bases for the corporate practice of medicine doctrine. However, in a subsequent 1994 act the Ohio legislature stated, in an uncodified provision, that nothing in Senate Bill 74 "shall alter or affect the law with respect to the practice of medicine and surgery or osteopathic medicine and surgery" (Ohio Amended Substitute Senate Bill No. 191, 1994).

According to Bill Schmidt, an attorney with Ohio's Medical Board, the board has interpreted Senate Bill No. 191 as preserving the corporate practice of medicine doctrine.[116] Consequently, the board has taken the position that physicians may not practice in any corporate form other than a professional association.

It could be argued, however, that if the legislature had intended to deny the business corporation form to physicians, it would have explicitly amended the corporations statute to that effect, rather than merely including its limitation in an uncodified provision not added to the Ohio statutes. Interestingly, the corporations division of the secretary of state's office is apparently not aware of Senate Bill 191 and has interpreted the revised statutory language to allow physicians to form business corporations.[117] Nevertheless, given that the medical board, not the corporations division, is responsible for enforcing the corporate practice of medicine doctrine, there is a real risk to any physicians forming a business corporation.

There is no comparable corporate practice of psychology doctrine that would prohibit psychologists from offering services through a business corporation. As noted, Senate Bill No. 74 provides that business corporations may now practice "any profession," and Senate Bill No. 191 attempted to limit Senate Bill No. 74 only with respect to the practice of medicine and osteopathy, not psychology. Vickie Hedges, the psychology board's enforcement supervisor, stated that the board does not have any rules restricting the corporate forms in which psychologists may practice.[118]

Thus, although psychologists would not be restricted and an argument could be made for the continued viability of the corporate practice of medicine doctrine, a multidisciplinary business corporation could create significant risks for any physician participants.[119]

Under the PA statute, which allows professionals to incorporate, physicians and psychologists clearly would not be permitted to jointly form a PA. The Ohio statutes define a PA as "an association organized . . . for the *sole purpose* of rendering *one* of the professional services authorized under" the professional licensure statutes (Ohio Rev. Code Ann. § 1785.01(B)). Furthermore, a PA may be organized and owned only by an individual or group of individuals "each of whom is licensed or otherwise legally authorized to render *the same kind of professional service*" (Ohio Rev. Code Ann. § 1785.02). Ms. Phipps confirmed that these statutes would prohibit physicians and psychologists from forming or practicing in a PA, even if the shareholders were all licensed in one discipline and hired practitioners in the other discipline to provide additional services.

## C. LLCs

Like the PA statute, Ohio LLC statute precludes the practice of multiple disciplines. Although the statute provides that an LLC may be formed for any lawful purpose *or purposes*, it also provides that in carrying out those purposes an LLC may "[r]ender *a* professional service" (Ohio Rev. Code Ann. §§ 1705.02, 1705.03(c)(6), Supp. 1994). Ms. Phipps confirmed that the corporations division interprets these provisions to preclude the formation and operation of LLCs that provide more than one type of professional service, regardless of whether services are provided through members or employees.[120] Moreover, because the LLC act was enacted in Senate Bill No. 74 (and therefore limited by Senate Bill No. 191), the Board of Medicine has taken the position that even physicians alone may not form LLCs.

## D. Networks

Ohio does not regulate physician networks or have an IPA or PPO statute. However, any network of physicians, psychologists, and allied health professionals would have to be structured so as to avoid violation of the medical practice act's fee-splitting prohibition.

## OKLAHOMA

### A. *Partnerships*

An Oklahoma partnership may be formed to engage in "every trade, occupation, or profession" (Okla. Stat. Ann. tit. 54, § 202). Neither the partnership laws nor the professional licensing laws impose any limitations on the ability of licensees in different professions to practice together. Psychologists, physicians, and allied health professionals may practice as partners and employees of a partnership, which may bill for their services.

Oklahoma law does not provide for LLPs.

### B. *Corporations*

No Oklahoma statute or case law prohibits the practice of medicine by a business corporation. Daniel Gamino, a private attorney who serves as counsel to the state medical board, explained that no such prohibition has been enforced in Oklahoma.[121] From the perspective of the board, any form of business association may employ physicians as long as the individuals rendering the services are duly licensed. Inasmuch as the psychology board also does not impose a prohibition on the corporate practice of psychology, according to board counsel Joe McCormick, it appears that physicians and psychologists may practice jointly as employees of a single business corporation.[122]

Under Oklahoma's PC act, a PC may be organized "only for the purpose of rendering one specific type of professional service or related professional services and services ancillary thereto and shall not engage in any business other than rendering the professional service or services" (Okla. Stat. Ann. tit. 18, § 806). The statute lists certain "related professionals" in the health care occupations who may combine to organize PCs; physicians and psychologists are included in the list (Okla. Stat. Ann. tit. 18, § 803). A PC is thus an acceptable form of organization for an Oklahoma multidisciplinary practice, as Mr. Gamino and Mr. McCormick agreed.[123]

## C. LLCs

Oklahoma's LLC act does not specifically address LLCs for the provision of professional services. It permits LLCs to conduct business in the state for any lawful business other than banking or insurance and specifies that the term "business" includes "any trade, occupation, profession or other activity" (Okla. Stat. Ann. tit. 18, §§ 2001(3), 2002). It thus appears that LLCs may render professional services. As to multidisciplinary LLCs, the use of the singular term "profession" implies that only a single profession may be rendered by an LLC. On the other hand, the fact that multidisciplinary PCs are permitted suggests that the same rule should apply to LLCs. The counsel to the respective professional boards indicated that they have not taken formal positions on this question and could not offer any guidance.[124] Thus, it is not clear whether a joint physician/psychologist LLC is a viable option in Oklahoma.

## D. Networks

Oklahoma does not regulate provider networks. Psychologists, physicians, and allied health professionals may form networks and contract with third-party payers to provide services.

## OREGON

### A. Partnerships

An Oregon partnership may be formed to engage in "every trade, occupation, or profession" (Oreg. Rev. Stat. § 58.076(2)). Neither the partnership laws nor the professional licensing laws impose any limitations on the ability of licensees in different professions to practice together. Psychologists, physicians, and allied health professionals may practice as partners and employees of a partnership, which may bill for their services.

Oregon enacted an LLP law in 1995 (Oreg. Rev. Stat. § 68.110). It specifically permits an LLP to "render professional service," without further addressing whether an LLP can render two types of professional services. Neither Lynn Rosik, the assistant attorney general who advises the secretary of state's office, or the counsel to the medical and psychology boards, could give guidance as to whether a multidisciplinary LLP is permissible.[125] It is therefore unclear whether the LLP form may be used for joint practice.

## B. *Corporations*

According to the Oregon business corporation act, "[a] business that is subject to regulation under another statute of [the] state may not be incorporated under this chapter if such business is required to be organized under such other statute" (Oreg. Rev. Stat. § 60.074(2)). Although Oregon does have a PC statute, it does not specify whether professionals desiring to incorporate their practices are "required" to use the PC form. As such, the statutory language does not provide a clear answer to whether incorporation as a business corporation is permissible.

Paul Sundermier, counsel to the Oregon Board of Medical Examiners, indicated that the only available legal guidance relating to the corporate practice of medicine of which the board is aware is contained in a 1947 case, *State ex rel. Sisemore v. Standard Optical Co. of Oregon* (188 P.2d 309, Ore. 1947).[126] In that case the court held that a business corporation's employment of an optometrist violated the optometry practice laws and implied that physicians would be subject to the same restriction. Mr. Sundermier indicated that the board has not enforced the rule in recent years but could not say that it was no longer valid. With respect to psychologists, there is no prohibition on practicing through an Oregon corporation, according to Bonnie Wilson, administrator of the Board of Psychologist Examiners.[127] Nevertheless, the unsettled state of the corporate practice of medicine doctrine makes it uncertain whether a business corporation may carry on a joint practice.

An Oregon PC may be formed "for the purpose of rendering professional service or services within two or more professions, and for the purpose of engaging in any lawful business . . . to the extent the combination of professional purposes or of professional and business purposes is expressly authorized by the regulatory board in [the] state applicable to each profession in the combination" (Oreg. Rev. Stat. § 58.076(2)). Ms. Wilson indicated that her board has approved such a combination in the past and does not regard it as problematic.[128] Mr. Sundermier was not able to say whether the medical board had addressed this particular combination, but he indicated that it has not rejected any of the combinations that have been proposed to it and doubted that one would be rejected unless it was "bizarre."[129] It thus appears that physicians and psychologists may carry on a joint practice by using the PC form in Oregon. It should be noted that at least one shareholder and one director of a PC must be licensed to render each professional service specified in the PC's articles of incorporation (Oreg. Rev. Stat. § 58.108(3), (4)).

## C. LLCs

In 1995 the Oregon legislature acted to permit LLCs to render professional services (Oreg. Rev. Stat. § 63.074(2)). The legislation contained the proviso that the practice is "subject to the laws of [the] state, the rules and regulations of the regulatory board of the profession, if any, and the standards of professional conduct of the profession, if any" As noted earlier, the boards of medicine and psychology do not consider joint medical/psychological practice barred, so it appears that a joint LLC may be an option in Oregon. However, until the boards address this question directly in the LLC context, this conclusion is not certain.

## D. Networks

Oregon regulates "health care service contractors" but imposes no limitations on the ability of different classes of mental health care providers to form networks. Psychologists, physicians, and allied health professionals may form such networks and contract with third-party payers to provide services.

## PENNSYLVANIA

## A. Partnerships

Under Pennsylvania law, partnerships may be formed to carry on any business, including "every trade, occupation or profession," subject to any other statute or regulation governing the particular business (15 Pa. C.S.A. §§ 103, 8102, 8302, 8311). The statutes and regulations governing the practice of medicine and psychology impose no such limitation on joint practices. April McClaine, Counsel to the Board of Medicine, confirms that the bureau routinely approves physician/psychologist partnerships.[130] Joint practice through employment agreements also is permissible, she advised. The partnership form is thus available for this practice combination in Pennsylvania.

Under state law, an LLP is treated the same as a general partnership for the purpose of determining whether it is a permissible entity for the practice of a profession (15 Pa. C.S.A. § 8201(c)(1)). It follows that the LLP form, like a partnership, allows licensees in medicine and psychology to practice together as partners or employees. Ms. McClaine concurred with this view.[131]

## B. Corporations

The law regarding the practice of medicine by Pennsylvania business corporations is uncertain. Although no Pennsylvania courts have addressed the issue in the medical context, a 1938 state supreme court case barred a corporation from employing optometrists, relying on a Massachusetts corporate practice of medicine case (Neill et al. v. Gimbel Brothers, Inc., 330 Pa. 213, 1938, citing *McMurdo v. Getter*, 298 Mass. 363, 1937). In the past the Pennsylvania Board of Medicine has cited the *Neill* case as grounds for the position that business corporations may not employ physicians. However, it appears that the board recently retreated from this stance. A January 19, 1995, letter from the board, written by Ms. McClaine in her capacity as board counsel, appears to attempt to relax the doctrine. The letter does not describe the particular facts of the situation but does make it clear that the correspondent had raised concerns about corporate practice. The board responded with the following statement:

> Medical care for the public in the Commonwealth must be provided by Pennsylvania licensed physicians. The independent professional judgments of such physicians relative to the diagnosis and treatment of disease or any ailment of the human body may not be controlled by unlicensed entities. Medical services may, however, be offered through relationships among physicians and entities whose purpose is the delivery of health and medical care to the public and who are regulated by a governmental body where the regulation requires licensed physician control over medical care decisions.[132]

Although the last sentence is somewhat obscure, Ms. McClaine explained that the board's intention was to permit corporate employment of physicians as long as the physicians maintain control of medical decisions. Thus, it appears that corporate employment of physicians is permitted under current board enforcement policy, but it must be noted that Ms. McClaine's letter does not have the force of law and analysis of any particular situation would depend on its facts. As to psychologists, Lois Fager of the Board of Psychology confirmed that there is no bar on their employment by a business corporation.[133]

In general, a Pennsylvania PC "may be incorporated only for the purpose of rendering one specific kind of professional service" (15 Pa. C.S.A. § 2903(c)). However, the PC statute allows incorporation of PCs to practice more than one profession, where

(i) the several shareholders of the professional corporation, if organized as a partnership, could conduct a combined practice of such specific kinds of professional services; or

(ii) the court, department, board, commission or other government unit regulating each profession involved in the professional corporation has by rule or regulation applicable to professional corporations expressly authorized the combined practice of the profession with each other profession involved in the regulation. (15 Pa. C.S.A. § 2903(d)(1))

As noted above, a joint physician/psychologist partnership is permissible in Pennsylvania, satisfying the first alternative. The second is satisfied as well. According to Board of Medicine's regulations, physicians may form PCs with "other health care practitioners who treat human ailments and conditions" if the other profession's supervisory board permits the combination (49 Pa. Code § 16.21). The Board of Psychology in its regulations expressly permits psychologists to form PCs with certain professionals, including medical doctors, if the incorporation is otherwise authorized under state regulations (49 Pa. Code § 41.26(a)). It thus appears that physicians and psychologists may practice as coshareholders of a Pennsylvania PC. Ms. McClaine confirmed this conclusion.[134] Although the relevant provisions do not specifically address employment relationships, Ms. McClaine explained that the practice boards would permit employment of either category of professional by a PC with shareholders in the other profession. PCs are clearly a viable form for multidisciplinary practice in Pennsylvania.

## C. LLCs

Under the recently enacted LLC act, an LLC may carry on "any business that a partnership without limited partners may carry on" (15 Pa. C.S.A. § 8911(a)). An LLC that renders one or more "restricted professional services," a term defined to include both medicine and psychology, is designated a "restricted professional company" (15 Pa. C.S.A. §§ 8903, 8995(a)).

The statute does not explicitly authorize such LLCs to engage in the practice of more than one profession; however, it refers several times to LLCs that render one or more professional services, strongly implying that multidisciplinary LLCs are permitted (see 15 Pa. C.S.A. §§ 8903, 8995(d),

8996(c)(1)). Ms. McClaine indicated that the Bureau of Professional and Occupational Affairs regards LLCs no differently from partnerships, LLPs, and PCs for purposes of joint practice.[135] Thus, comembership of physicians and psychologists in an LLC, or their employment by an LLC, is permissible.

## D. Networks

The state's PPO statute, and the regulations promulgated thereunder by the Department of Insurance, do not impose limitations on provider network membership (40 Pa. C.S.A. § 764a et seq., 31 Pa. Code § 152.1 et seq.). Psychologists, physicians, and allied health professionals may form and contract with networks in Pennsylvania.

## RHODE ISLAND

### A. Partnerships

A Rhode Island partnership may be formed to engage in "every trade, occupation, or profession" (R.I. Gen. Laws § 7-12-13(b)). Neither the partnership laws nor the professional licensing laws impose any limitations on the ability of licensees in different professions to practice together. Psychologists, physicians, and allied health professionals may practice as partners and employees of a partnership, which may bill for their services.

Rhode Island law does not provide for LLPs.

### B. Corporations

Rhode Island law is not clear on the corporate employment of physicians. Neither statutory nor case law expressly prohibits the corporate practice of medicine. The Rhode Island Supreme Court has ruled that business corporations may not engage in the practice of law (*Carter v. Berberian*, 434 A.2d 255, R.I. 1981). Although the statute interpreted in the case was similar to the medical practice act, no court has addressed the issue in the medical context. Bruce McIntyre, legal advisor to the Board of Medical Licensure and Discipline, indicated that the board does not prohibit employment of physicians by business corporations.[136] Vanessa Picard of the Division of Professional Regulation, which regulates psychology, noted that her agency sees no problem with corporate employment of psychologists.[137] However, Katherine Merola, legal counsel to the secretary of state's office, indicated that it regards the PC form as the only one available for professional practice and thus would refuse to accept a filing for a business corporation if the application makes it clear that the corporation will employ professionals.[138] However, she acknowledged that no law explicitly imposes such a restriction and that such employment is in fact widespread. It thus appears that employment of physicians and psychologists by a business corporation may be permissible in Rhode Island, but this conclusion cannot be stated with certainty.

The state's PC law also is unclear. Rhode Island PCs "may engage in rendering professional services of not more than one of the professions enumerated in § 7-5.1-2" of the state laws (R.I. Gen. Laws § 7-5.1-3(a)). Every officer, director and shareholder must be licensed in that profession and employed by the PC in such practice. Unlike medicine, however, psychology is not among the professions listed in section 7-5.1-2. The statute further obliges each PC to render its professional services only through employees who are authorized to practice, but specifies that PCs are not precluded "from employing unlicensed persons to perform functions not constituting professional services" (R.I. Gen. Laws § 7-5.1-6). Since psychologists are professionals who require state licensure but are not listed as providers of "professional services," application of this provision to them is not clear. The statutory language does support the argument that, since psychologists do not provide "professional services" within the statutory definition, they may practice as PC employees. Ms. Merola expressed doubt about this conclusion, however.[139] It thus appears possible, but not certain, that the PC act would permit a multidisciplinary physician/psychologist practice in which the physicians are the PC shareholders and the psychologists are employees.

## C. LLCs

The Rhode Island LLC act permits formation of an LLC for the purpose of engaging in any business that a limited partnership may carry on "except the provision of professional services, as defined in § 7-5.1-2" (R.I. Gen. Laws § 7-16-3). As noted above, the section cited does not include psychological practice but does expressly include medical practice. Although an LLC could be formed to practice psychology, it seems that the employment of physicians by such an LLC would not be permissible. The LLC is thus not an option for a joint practice in Rhode Island.

## D. Networks

Rhode Island does not regulate provider networks. Psychologists, physicians, and allied health professionals may form networks and contract with third-party payers to provide services.

## SOUTH CAROLINA

### A. Partnerships

There do not appear to be any statutory barriers to multidisciplinary partnerships in South Carolina. Psychologists, physicians, and allied health professionals may practice as partners and employees of a partnership. A partnership may bill third-party payers for the professional services of its partners and employees.

South Carolina recently enacted an LLP statute (1994 S.C. Act 448). It permits professional LLPs and does not impose any single-discipline limitations. Thus, physicians and psychologists may practice jointly in a South Carolina LLP.

### B. Corporations

In 1948 the South Carolina Supreme Court indicated that business corporations may not employ physicians to practice medicine (*Wadsworth v. McRae Drug Co.*, 28 S.E.2d 417). A 1966 opinion by the state attorney general reaffirmed the prohibition (Op. Atty. Gen., S.C. A.G. Lexis 127, June 20). However, Rick Wilson, counsel to the Board of Medical Examiners, indicated that the board no longer enforces the prohibition.[140] According to Mr. Wilson, the board is only interested in a physician business arrangement if it negatively affects patient care. Based on this enforcement stance, it appears that in South Carolina physicians may practice as shareholders or employees of a business corporation. There is also no prohibition on the corporate practice of psychology. There is no statute or regulation generally prohibiting multidisciplinary practices, and the counsel to the relevant practice boards saw no problem with such arrangements.[141] It thus appears that a physician/psychologist business corporation may be formed in South Carolina.

PCs in South Carolina are limited to "the rendering of professional services, including services ancillary to them, within a single profession" (S.C. Code Ann. § 33-19-110(a)). A PC may not engage in any business other than the professional service and business authorized by its articles of incorporation (S.C. Code Ann. § 33-19-140(a)). An exception to this single-profession rule exists "to the extent [that] the combination of professional purposes . . . is authorized by the licensing law of [the] State applicable to each profession in the combination" (S.C. Code Ann. § 33-19-110(b)). Mr. Wilson, counsel also to the Board of Medical Examiners, explained that the board makes this determination on a case-by-case basis but that approval is routinely given.[142] Patti Glenn, of the Board of Psychology Examiners, indicated that her board takes the same view.[143] It thus appears that a PC in which both physicians and psychologists hold shares, or with shareholders in one profession and employees in another, is a viable option in South Carolina.

## C. LLCs

The South Carolina LLC act permits organization of LLCs for the provision of professional services (S.C. Code Ann. § 33-43-1101(A)). Like the PC statute, the LLC law generally limits LLCs to a single profession and bars the professional LLC from engaging in other business activities (S.C. Code Ann. § 33-43-1104(A)). The exception, once again, is that LLCs may engage in additional professions to the extent that the combination is authorized by the professional licensure laws (S.C. Code Ann. § 33-43-1104(B)). As noted above, the medicine and psychology boards routinely approve professional combinations, and a physician/psychologist combination would likely be permitted. The LLC form is therefore likely to be available for a multidisciplinary practice.

## D. Networks

Psychologists, physicians, and allied health professionals may form and contract with networks in South Carolina.

## SOUTH DAKOTA

## A. Partnerships

A South Dakota partnership may be formed to engage in "every trade, occupation, or profession" (S.D. Codified Laws Ann. § 48-1-1(2)). Neither the partnership laws nor the professional licensing laws impose any limitations on the ability of licensees in different professions to practice together. Psychologists, physicians, and allied health professionals may practice as partners and employees of a partnership, which may bill for their services.

South Dakota's LLP act took effect July 1, 1995. It specifies that any person licensed pursuant to certain statutory chapters may practice in an LLP (S.D. Codified Laws Ann. § 48-7-11). Although the medical licensure chapter is among those listed, the psychology licensing chapter is not. And although the provision does not explicitly prohibit members of other professions from practicing in an LLP, the omission of any mention of them implies that they are barred. Sherry Sundem-Wald, the deputy attorney general who advises the secretary of state, agrees.[144] Thus LLPs do not appear to be an option for multidisciplinary mental health practices in South Dakota.

### B. *Corporations*

A South Dakota statute enacted in 1993 expressly prohibits corporations from practicing medicine (S.D. Codified Laws Ann. § 36-4-8.1); however, it qualifies this rule as follows:

> A corporation is not engaged in the practice of medicine. . . by entering into an employment agreement with a physician licensed pursuant to this chapter if the agreement or the relationship it creates does not:

> (1) In any manner, directly or indirectly, supplant, diminish or regulate the physician's independent judgment concerning the practice of medicine or the diagnosis and treatment of any patient;

> (2) Result in profit to the corporation from the practice of medicine itself, such as by the corporation charging a greater fee for the physician's services than which he would otherwise reasonably charge as an independent practitioner, except that the corporation may make additional charges reasonably associated with the services rendered, such as facility, equipment, or administrative charges; and

(3) Remain effective for a period of more than three years, after which it may be renewed by both parties annually.

There is no similar prohibition in the psychology practice laws. There is also no general ban on physicians and psychologists practicing jointly, according to Sharvin Dixon, director of the Board of Medical and Osteopathic Examiners, and Carol Tellinghuysen of the Board of Psychology.[145] It thus appears that a business corporation that meets the requirements quoted above may conduct a joint mental health practice through employed physicians and psychologists.

In contrast to the majority of states, which have a single PC statute that applies to all professions, South Dakota law makes a variety of corporations available to particular professions. Although there is no provision for a psychology corporation, "medical corporations" (MCs) may be organized (S.D. Codified Laws Ann. § 47-11-1). Only licensed physicians may be officers, directors, or shareholders of an MC, so it is clear that physicians and psychologists may not jointly own an MC (S.D. Codified Laws Ann. § 47-11-3). Employment of members of a second profession, however, appears to comport with the statute:

> One or more persons licensed pursuant to . . . the Medical Practice Act may associate to form a corporation pursuant to the provisions of law pertaining to private corporations to own, operate and maintain an establishment for the study, diagnosis and treatment of human ailments and injuries, *whether physician or mental* . . . and for any other purpose incident or necessary thereto; provided *medical or surgical* treatment, consultation or advice may be given by employees of the corporation only if they are licensed pursuant to the Medical Practice Act. (S.D. Codified Laws Ann. § 47-11-1, emphases added).

By expressly including mental health among the purposes of an MC, while requiring medical licensure only for persons providing medical or surgical treatment, the statute appears to permit other types of mental health professionals, such as psychologists, to practice as employees of an MC. Neither Mr. Dixon nor Ms. Tellinghuysen disagreed with this conclusion.[146] Such an arrangement therefore appears to be a viable option in South Dakota.

## C. LLCs

In South Dakota an LLC may be organized for any lawful purpose except banking or insurance; however, LLCs are subject to the restrictions found in the various professional corporation laws (including the MC law) and "any other restrictions by law" (S.D. Codified Laws Ann. § 47-34-5). This proviso appears to mean that medical licensees may organize LLCs only if they observe the restrictions of the MC law, including the requirement that only physicians have equity interests. In addition, the MC statute expressly includes LLCs in its definition of corporations, making all the provisions of the MC statute applicable to medical LLCs (S.D. Codified Laws Ann. § 47-11-1.1(1)). Thus, the conclusion reached above with respect to MCs—that they may employ psychologists but may have only physician owners—would apply to LLCs also. Once again, the personnel from the practice boards were not aware of any limitations that would contradict this conclusion.[147] Psychologists may thus practice as employees of a physician-owned LLC.

## D. Networks

South Dakota does not regulate provider networks. Psychologists, physicians, and allied health professionals may form networks and contract with third-party payers to provide services.

## TENNESSEE

## A. Partnerships

A Tennessee partnership may be formed to engage in "every trade, occupation, or profession" (Tenn. Code Ann. § 61-1-101(2)). Neither the partnership laws nor the professional licensing laws impose any limitations on the ability of licensees in different professions to practice together. Psychologists, physicians, and allied health professionals may practice as partners and employees of a partnership, which may bill for their services.

Tennessee enacted an LLP law in 1995, and professional LLPs are explicitly permitted (1995 Tenn. S.B. 193, § 10). Multidisciplinary professional LLPs are not addressed, but the law does affirm that LLPs are subject to the conditions imposed by professional licensure authorities. As discussed below, the Tennessee Department of Health has proposed regulations that would prohibit multidisciplinary PCs or LLCs, including physicians. Although the regulations do not currently address LLPs, since the LLP form is so new, they could be modified to do so, and the department's apparent intent is to prohibit all joint practices. Although it appears that a physician/psychologist LLP is permitted at this time, it is uncertain whether this will continue to be the case.

## B. Corporations

The prohibition on the employment of physicians by a business corporation continues to be enforced in Tennessee. In a 1988 opinion the attorney general endorsed a 1949 case barring the practice of "learned professions" by business corporations and concluded that this bar applied to the medical profession (Op. Tenn. Atty. Gen. No. 88-152, August 25), *citing State ex rel. Loser v. National Optical Stores Co.*, 225 S.W.2d 263, Tenn. 1949). The Tennessee doctrine is particularly extreme in its scope, as the attorney general more recently opined that the doctrine extends to a corporation's employment of physicians to treat its employees at no charge (Op. Tenn. Atty. Gen. No. 94-009, January 28, 1994) and to physician employment by nonprofit hospitals and public benefit corporations (Op. Tenn. Atty. Gen. No. 94-53, April 12, 1994). A 1995 statute permits only hospitals to employ physicians (1995 Tenn. H.B. 712). In light of Tennessee's strict rule, a business corporation is not a viable approach for a multidisciplinary practice there.

According to the state's PC act, a corporation may elect PC status

for the purpose of rendering professional service within two (2) or more professions, and for the purpose of engaging in any lawful business authorized by the Tennessee Business Corporation Act, only if the combination of professional purposes or of professional and business purposes is specifically authorized by the licensing law of [the] state applicable to each profession in the combination. (Tenn. Code Ann. § 48-3-605(b))

Recently adopted PC regualtions, however, specifically prohibit physicians from holding shares in PCs with nonphysicians (Tenn. Comp. R. & Regs. 0880-8-1 *et seq.*). An attorney for the Department of Health indicated that his office also interprets the rule to bar physican PCs from employing a second type of professional.[148] The PC form is thus not an option in Tennessee.

## C. LLCs

The Tennessee LLC act specifically provides for the organization of PLLCs to render professional services. Combinations of professions are permitted in the same circumstances as under the PC act (Tenn. Code Ann. § 48-248-104(b)). Mr. Kramer explained that the Department of Health has proposed rules for physician participation in LLCs that are identical to those for PCs.[149] If the proposed rules are adopted, the LLC form will thus not be available for multidisciplinary practices in Tennessee.

## D. Networks

Tennessee does not regulate provider networks, with the exception of networks that provide services through the state's TennCare program. According to Bill Young, deputy commissioner of the Department of Commerce and Insurance, the governor has signed an executive order requiring TennCare contractors, such as PPOs, to register with the department.[150] He noted that such networks are not subject to any limitations on their provider membership. Psychologists, physicians, and allied health professionals may thus form networks and contract with third-party payers to provide services.

## TEXAS

## A. Partnerships

There do not appear to be any barriers to multidisciplinary general partnerships of individual practitioners under Texas law. Psychologists, physicians, and allied health professionals may practice as partners and employees of a partnership. The partnership may bill third-party payers for the professional services of its partners and employees.

Texas law also authorizes LLPs. The LLP statute does not impose any restrictions that would bar professionals from organizing as a multidisciplinary LLP (Texas Rev. Civ. Stat. Ann. art. 6132b-3.08).

## B. Corporations

The corporate practice of medicine doctrine remains vital in Texas, preventing business corporations from rendering any physician services.

For a physician to "aid or abet" an unlicensed entity in the practice of medicine is grounds for disciplinary action (Texas Rev. Civ. Stat. Ann. art. 4495b, § 3.08 (15)).

An exception to the prohibition exists for nonprofit corporations "formed solely by" physicians for certain purposes, including "the delivery of health care to the public" (Texas Rev. Civ. Stat. Ann. art. 4495b, § 5.01 (a)). Texas law requires that such organizations be organized and incorporated by physicians and that the directors and trustees of the organizations be actively engaged in the practice of medicine (Texas Rev. Civ. Stat. Ann. art. 4495b, § 5.01 (a)(3)). However, it appears that other health care professionals, such as psychologists, may practice as employees of such a corporation.

The state's professional corporation act appears to allow psychologists to form PCs. However, the statute limits all PCs to "one specific type of professional service" (Texas Rev. Civ. Stat. Ann. art. 1528e, § 6). Multidisciplinary PCs are clearly not viable under Texas law.

Physicians in Texas may not form PCs (Texas Rev. Civ. Stat. Ann. art. 1528e, § 3(a)). Texas law does authorize physicians to organize in the form of a professional association (PA), which shares certain characteristics with PCs (Texas Rev. Civ. Stat. Ann. art. 1528f, § 24). Nevertheless, the PA form is available only for groups performing a single professional service, and each member must be licensed in that profession (Texas Rev. Civ. Stat. Ann. art. 1528f, § 2). Psychologists and physicians therefore could not be members of a PA together.

## C. LLCs

It appears that the formation of an LLC that includes physicians is prohibited in Texas. The LLC statute reads, in part, as follows:

A limited liability company engaging in a business that is subject to regulation by another Texas statute may be formed under this Act only if it is not prohibited by the other statute. The limited liability company is subject to all limitations of the other statute (Texas Rev. Civ. Stat. Ann. art. 1528n, § 2.01(B)).

Although the ban on the corporate practice of medicine is not statutory, it is enforced through the statutory ban on aiding or abetting the unlicensed practice of medicine noted above (Texas Rev. Civ. Stat. Ann. art. 4495b,

§ 3.08 (15)). While not certain, it appears that medical practice by an LLC would thus not be permissible under the LLC act.

Texas authorizes PLLCs but provides that they "may not render more than one kind of professional service" (Texas Rev. Civ. Stat. Ann. art. 1528n, § 11.01(A)(2)). Practitioners of different types of health care thus may not establish a PLLC under Texas law.

### D. Networks

Texas does not specifically regulate networks. State regulations make clear, however, that hospitals and state-certified HMOs may contract with both physicians and other providers (including mental health professionals) for the provision of services (Texas Ins. Code Ann. arts. 20.11, 20A.06(a)(3); 25 Texas Admin. Code §119.9(f)(1)). Thus, a network with both physician and psychologist members could enter into such contracts.

## UTAH

### A. Partnerships

A partnership may be formed in Utah to carry on a business, including "every trade, occupation, or profession" (Utah Code Ann. § 48-1-48). The state's medical practice act, however, imposes a significant limitation on physicians practicing in partnerships:

> "Unprofessional conduct" . . . includes . . . practicing medicine as a partner, agent, or employee of, or in joint venture with, any person who does not hold a license to practice medicine in this state. . . . (Utah Code Ann. § 58-12-28(5)(f)).

Thus, physicians may not practice as partners with other professionals, such as psychologists; Ray Walker, counsel to the Division of Professional Licensing of the Department of Commerce, confirmed this conclusion.[151] Although the provision's language suggests that physicians also are precluded from serving as employees of partnerships that include nonphysician partners, Mr. Walker indicated that such an arrangement might be permissible but that case-by-case analysis would be necessary. The statute does not prohibit physicians from employing nonphysicians, however, and the psychologist licensing act does not preclude the employment of psychologists by nonpsychologist partnerships. It thus appears that a multidisciplinary practice may be accomplished by having psychologists as employees of a partnership of physicians.

Utah's 1994 LLP statute permits professional LLPs (Utah Code Ann. § 48-1-48(1)). However, such an LLP is restricted to "one specific type of professional service," thereby precluding physician/psychologist partnerships. An LLP also "may not engage in any business other than rendering the professional service that it was organized to render." Therefore, an LLP organized to practice one profession may not employ members of a second profession. George Daniels, counsel to the Division of Corporations and Commercial Code of the Department of Commerce, confirmed that multidisciplinary LLPs are not a viable option.[152]

## B. *Corporations*

Business corporations in Utah may engage in "any lawful business" subject to any limitations found in the statutes regulating the business (Utah Code Ann. § 16-10a-301). The PC act does not expressly preclude incorporation by professionals as a business corporation if the professionals would be permitted to render services through such a corporation "in the absence of this act" (Utah Code Ann. § 16-11-15). Mr. Walker noted, however, that the Division of Professional Licensing of the Department of Commerce has challenged some cases of the corporate practice of medicine on the grounds that the physician, as an employee of a "person who does not hold a license to practice medicine," has engaged in "unprofessional conduct" within the meaning of state law (Utah Code Ann. § 58-12-28(5)(f)).[153] He indicated that there is not a specific prohibition on employment of physicians but that factors which may make a particular arrangement not permissible include corporate control of a physician's medical judgment and fee splitting by the physician and corporation. A business corporation's employment of psychologists is less likely to pose difficulties. In general, it appears that employment of physicians and psychologists by a business corporation is permitted in Utah, but the lack of clear rules regarding such an arrangement keeps such an arrangement from being an optimal choice for a multidisciplinary practice.

Both medicine and psychology are listed among the professional services in which a Utah PC may engage (Utah Code Ann. § 16-11-2). Like an LLP, a PC is limited to a single profession (Utah Code Ann. § 16-11-6). The PC's shareholders, officers, and directors must be licensed to render the same service (Utah Code Ann. § 16-11-8). Physicians and psychologists may therefore not be coshareholders in a Utah PC. Subject only to an exception not relevant here, a PC is further precluded from "engag[ing] in any business other than rendering the professional service which it was organized to render and services ancillary thereto" (Utah Code Ann. § 16-11-6). Thus, a PC organized to practice one profession, such as psychology, may not hire as employees members of a second profession, such as medicine. These views are shared by the Division of Corporations and Commercial Code of the Department of Commerce, according to Mr. Daniels.[154]

## C. LLCs

The provisions of Utah's LLC act relevant to multidisciplinary practices are identical to those of the LLP and PC acts, discussed above. Professional LLCs are permitted, but may render only one specific type of professional service (Utah Code Ann. § 48-2b-105(2)). Accordingly, joint physician/psychologist membership in an LLC is barred. A professional LLC is also precluded from engaging in any business other than rendering the services it was organized to render. Thus, employment of members of a second profession by an LLC is not permissible. Mr. Daniels reported that the Division of Corporations concurs.[155]

## D. Networks

Utah law does not restrict provider networks. Psychologists, physicians, and allied health professionals may form and contract with networks in the state.

## VERMONT

### A. Partnerships

A partnership may be formed in Vermont to carry on a business, including "every trade, occupation, or profession" (Vermont Stat. Ann., tit. 11, §§ 1121, 1161). The statutes regulating the practice of medicine and psychology do not prohibit members of the respective professions from practicing as partners of other types of professionals. Sienna Walton and John Chase, counsels to the medicine and psychology practice boards, respectively, confirmed that multidisciplinary partnerships are permissible.[156] Psychologists, physicians, and allied health professionals may practice as partners and employees of a partnership, which may bill for their services.

Vermont does not have an LLP statute.

## B. *Corporations*

Under Vermont law, business corporations may generally engage in "any lawful business" (Vermont Stat. Ann., tit. 11A, § 3.01); however, corporations engaging in a business regulated under another state law may incorporate only if permitted by, and subject to any limitations of, the other statute. The fact that the state's PC act is listed as one such statute effectively implies that PCs are the only corporate form available for professional practice. Although Vermont's medical practice board approved employment of physicians by a nonprofit corporation in a 1994 declaratory ruling, the secretary of state appears to take a different view. John Chase, an attorney with the secretary of state's office responsible for corporate law issues, confirmed that his office regards the employment of either physicians or psychologists by a business corporation as not permissible.[157]

A Vermont PC may provide only "one specific type of professional service," and its shareholders, officers, and directors must be licensed to render that same service (Vermont Stat. Ann., tit. 11, §§ 804, 806). Accordingly, physicians and psychologists may not be coshareholders in a Vermont PC. Because PCs are barred from engaging in any business other than professional service it was organized to render and ancillary services, a PC organized to practice one profession, such as psychology, may not employ members of a second profession, such as medicine. Mr. Chase agreed with these conclusions.[158]

## C. LLCs

Vermont does not have an LLC statute; its legislature did not pass a proposed one during the 1995 session.

## D. *Networks*

Vermont does not impose limitations on provider networks. Physicians, psychologists, and allied health professionals may form and contract with networks in the state.

## VIRGINIA

### A. *Partnerships*

Virginia law appears to pose no barriers to multidisciplinary partnerships. Psychologists, physicians, and allied health professionals may practice as partners and employees of a partnership. The partnership may bill third-party payers for the professional services of its partners and employees.

The Virginia LLP statute makes no reference to professional LLPs, but it also does not impose any limitation on the permissible purposes of an LLP (Va. Code. Ann. § 50-43.1 *et seq.*). Sandra Thompson of the Virginia Corporation Commission confirmed that physicians and psychologists may practice jointly as partners in a Virginia LLP and that an LLP with partners of one profession may employ members of a second profession.[159]

### B. *Corporations*

The Virginia attorney general acknowledged in a 1992 opinion that no Virginia case or statute imposes a prohibition on the employment of physicians by business corporations (Op. Atty. Gen., Va. AG Lexis 66, December 7). The facts presented to the attorney general involved employment of physicians by a nonprofit hospital. The attorney general also discussed physician employment by business corporations, concluding that such relationships are legal if the employment agreement "authorizes the physician to exercise control over the diagnosis and treatment of the patient." The opinion did not mention two cases in which, under similar statutes, other professionals' relationships with business corporations were held to constitute unlawful practice of those professions (*Virginia Beach S.P.C.A., Inc. v. South Hampton Roads Veterinary Assoc.*, 229 Va. 349, 1985, veterinary medicine; *Ritholz v. Commonwealth*, 184 Va. 339, 1945, optometry). Nevertheless, Lynn Fleming, the assistant attorney general who counsels the professional licensing boards, confirmed that the position of the attorney general's office is that business corporations may employ physicians.[160] She also confirmed that psychologists may be employed by a business corporation. Given that neither the professional licensure laws nor the business corporation laws prohibit a corporation from employing both psychologists and physicians, Ms. Fleming also agreed that such arrangements would be permissible.[161]

Under Virginia's PC act, persons duly licensed to render the "same professional services" may be coshareholders of a PC formed "for the sole and specific purpose of rendering the same and specific professional service" (Va. Code Ann. § 13.1-544). The definitions section of the law, however, deems a number of health-related professions to be the "same professional service" for purposes of the statute (Va. Code Ann. § 13.1-543(A)). Among these are the provision of services by licensed "practitioners of the healing arts," including physicians, and by licensed "practitioners of the behavioral science professions," including psychologists. The definition of "professional corporation" further makes it clear that "any combination" of the specified health care professionals may hold shares and practice in a single PC (Va. Code Ann. § 13.1-544(B)). It thus follows that in Virgina physicians and psychologists may practice jointly as shareholders of a PC; Emerson Wilbey, an attorney for the state corporation commission, agrees.[162]

As to employment relationships, another provision of Virginia law mandates that no PC

> may render professional services except through its officers, employees and agents who are duly licensed or otherwise legally authorized to render such professional services, and only shareholders, officers, employees, and agents licensed or otherwise legally qualified by this Commonwealth may perform the professional service. . . . (Va. Code Ann. § 13.1-546)

These provisions, along with the definition of "professional service," seem to indicate that a PC owned by one class of health care professional (e.g., psychologists) may employ licensed members of another health profession (e.g. physicians). This conclusion is subject to the limitations that the employed professionals be duly licensed and that their services be within the scope of the PC's statement of purposes. Mr. Wilbey indicated that the corporation commission would reach the same conclusion.[163]

In contrast to ownership or employment relationships, independent contractor relationships between professionals and PCs are barred in Virginia, even if the professional and the PC are authorized to practice the same profession. In *P. M. Palumbo, Jr., M.D., Inc. v. Bennett* (409 S.E.2d 152, Va. 1991), the Virginia Supreme Court addressed section 13.1-546, discussed above. In this case an orthopedic physician had entered into an "independent contractor agreement" with a PC formed to provide orthopedic medical and surgical services. After the physician terminated the contract, the PC sued to enforce certain restrictive covenants, and the physician answered that the contract was void and unenforceable. Relying on the language in section 13.1-546 that no PC "may render professional services except through its officers, employees and agents," the Virginia Supreme Court agreed with the physician's argument that "the contract violates Code § 13.1-546 because the statute does not allow a professional corporation to render professional services through an independent contractor" (409 S.E.2d at 153). As the attorney general noted regarding *Palumbo* in the 1992 opinion mentioned earlier, "[t]he Court apparently did not consider an independent contractor to be an 'agent' of the professional corporation for purposes of § 13.1-546 under the facts of that case" (1992 Va. AG Lexis 66).

Nonetheless, the court held that the contract was enforceable on the grounds that the relevant section of the PC act "was not intended to be an exercise of the Commonwealth's police power" (409 S.E. 2d at 154). The court emphasized that the law neither mentions contracts nor provides for penalties and followed earlier cases holding that a contract in violation of a statute is enforceable unless the law was "enacted to protect the public against fraud, imposition, or to safeguard the public health, or morals. . . . " Section 13.1-546 of the PC act is not such a statute, according to the court. This part of the holding creates some uncertainty as to application of the rule in situations other than enforcement of contracts. Even so, the court's clear statement that a Virginia PC may not render professional services through independent contractors would seem to limit PCs, including joint psychologist/physician PCs, to the coownership and employment models described above.

## C. LLCs

The sections of the Virginia PLLC act relevant to the permissibility of multidisciplinary groups mirror those of the PC act. Although PLLC membership is restricted to those performing the "same professional services" (§ 13.1-1103), the definitions of the terms "professional services" and "professional limited liability company" (§ 13.1-1102) clearly indicate that psychology and medicine are deemed to be the same professional services. Thus, physicians and psychologists may be comembers of a single PLLC.

A PLLC is constrained to render professional services only through its "members, managers, employees and agents who are duly licensed…" (§ 13.1-1107). As with PCs, it follows that employment of physicians by a psychologist-owned PLLC, or vice versa, is permissible. Mr. Wilbey confirmed these conclusions.[164]

Less clear is whether the *Palumbo* case would apply to PLLCs, thereby preventing them from entering into independent contractor relationships with professionals. Mr. Wilbey was unwilling to comment on this, and no certain answer can be given.[165] It is noteworthy that the language of the PLLC statute is virtually identical to that on which the *Palumbo* court relied and that the PLLC act was enacted in 1992, after the decision. Thus, there is a strong basis for concluding that a Virginia PLLC may not engage professionals, including either physicians or psychologists, to render professional services as independent contractors.

### D. Networks

Virginia does not impose limitations on provider networks. Networks of physicians, psychologists, and allied health professionals may thus contract with third-party payers for the provision of services.

## WASHINGTON

### A. Partnerships

Washington law appears not to allow partnerships of physicians and psychologists. Unlike most states, Washington subjects partnerships to its bar on the corporate practice of learned professions. The state supreme court thus refused to enforce a medical clinic partnership agreement in which ownership of the clinic was shared by a physician and a lay person (*Morelli v. Ehsan*, 756 P.2d 129, Wash. 1988). The court regarded it as "anomalous" to allow non-physicians to have an ownership interest in an entity that rendered medical services merely because they were partners rather than shareholders. It is possible that the court would be more inclined to accept a partnership between physicians and psychologists than one between physicians and persons who hold no professional license of any kind, but such an approach cannot be recommended at this time.

Washington has not enacted an LLP statute.

## B. *Corporations*

In accordance with state doctrine regarding the corporate practice of learned professions, a for-profit corporation may not employ, or bill for the services of, physicians or psychologists in Washington (*Morelli v. Ehsan*, 756 P.2d 129, 132, Wash. 1988). Nonprofit and professional corporations are exempt from the ban. Professionals may organize nonprofit corporations to provide professional services but are subject to the same limitations imposed on PCs (Wash. Rev. Code Ann. § 18.100.050).

Washington law does not permit multidisciplinary PCs. A 1980 opinion by the state attorney general held that PCs incorporated to provide medical services are barred from giving nonphysicians—specifically, licensed psychologists—stock ownership in the corporation. Nor may a PC organize itself with the purpose of providing a broad range of health care services and then admit licensees in the various health disciplines as stockholders (Op. Atty. Gen. 1980, L.O. No. 18).

The state legislature has created a narrow exception, allowing different types of professionals to organize in PCs to provide services to HMO enrollees (Wash. Rev. Code Ann. § 18.100.050). In general, however, professionals of different disciplines who wish to provide services to non-HMO enrollees may not do so through a single PC.

## C. LLCs

In light of the state supreme court's strict prohibition against the rendering of professional services by business corporations, it is unlikely that Washington authorities would allow professionals to provide services through LLCs other than PLLCs.

Washington does allow for the creation of PLLCs, and such entities would be a viable means of rendering medical or psychological services. However, the LLC statute does not appear to permit the formation of multidisciplinary PLLCs. The statute permits the formation of a PLLC by "persons engaged in *a* profession" if the managers and members are licensed to "practice *the* profession" (Wash. Rev. Code Ann. § 25.15.045(1), emphasis added). The most natural reading of these terms would limit PLLCs to a single profession. An attorney for the Corporations Division of the Office of the Secretary of State expressed disagreement with this interpretation.[166]

PLLCs are permitted to have PCs or other PLLCs as members if the member entity's relevant personnel meet the licensure requirements to provide the "same specific professional services" as the PLLC (Wash. Rev. Code Ann. § 25.15.045(5)).

## D. Networks

Multispecialty networks are permitted in Washington. Networks in the state are generally restricted to fee-for-service arrangements with third-party payers. A network that wants to enter into risk-bearing arrangements might seek licensure as a "health care service contractor" (HCSC). HCSCs must be "sponsored by or otherwise intimately connected with a provider or group of providers"; the providers need not be in the same discipline. HCSCs are permitted to contract on a prepaid basis with payers to provide "one or more health care services" through participating providers (Wash. Rev. Code Ann. § 48.44.020(1).10).

## WEST VIRGINIA

## A. Partnerships

A West Virginia partnership may be formed to engage in "every trade, occupation, or profession" (W. Va. Code § 47B-1-1). Neither the partnership laws nor the professional licensing laws impose any limitations on the ability of licensees in different professions to practice together. Psychologists, physicians, and allied health professionals may practice as partners and employees of a partnership, which may bill for their services.

West Virginia law does not provide for LLPs.

## B. Corporations

In two opinions during the 1950s the state attorney general indicated that in West Virginia the corporate practice of medicine is strictly prohibited (44 Op. Atty. Gen. W. Va. 5, 1950, employment of physician by a hospital barred; 46 Op. Atty. Gen. W. Va. 202, 1955, physician employment by an unlicensed person, association, or corporation barred). However, in May 1995 the West Virginia Board of Medicine issued a "Statement of Public Policy" on the corporate practice of medicine. The statement lists a number of factors relevant to the board's determination of whether, in a given case, a corporation that employs physicians is practicing medicine and thus violating state law. Factors supporting a finding that such an arrangement is permitted include the public benefit of the arrangement, the preservation of physician autonomy, nonprofit status of the corporation, and shareholder agreements protecting physicians from lawsuits for breach of fiduciary duties "where decisions are made by them in the best interests of medicine which may erode the profitability of the corporation." The board concluded that corporate employment of physicians is "not per se violative" of state law. Deborah Lewis Rodecker, legal counsel to the Board of Medicine, could not say whether the "nonprofit status" criterion is so firm that for-profit corporations are effectively barred.[167] The state's psychology practice act specifies that corporations may not render psychological services "except through a licensee or licensees," clearly implying that there is no prohibition on the corporate practice of psychology (W. Va. Code § 30-21-3(b)). If the conditions described in the board's statement are substantially met, it appears that employment by a business corporation is a viable option in West Virginia; if those conditions are met only in part, however, the conclusion is less certain.

West Virginia does not have a general PC act, but its medical practice act does allow one or more duly licensed physicians to form "medical corporations" (MCs) (W. Va. Code § 30-3-15(a)). The Board of Medicine must approve applications to set up MCs, and MCs may not practice medicine without a certificate of approval from the board (W. Va. Code § 30-3-15(a), (d)). MCs may render medical services through physicians who are either shareholders or employees (W. Va. Code § 30-3-15(b)). Because the law requires MCs to cease practicing medicine on notification by the board that a shareholder is no longer duly licensed, it is clear that nonphysicians, such as psychologists, may not be coowners of an MC (W. Va. Code § 30-3-15(c)). Ms. Rodecker indicated that the board considers this provision to preclude employment of a second type of professional by an MC.[168] It thus appears that MCs may not be used for a physician/psychologist practice in West Virginia.

## C. LLCs

West Virginia's LLC act does not specifically address the provision of professional services (W. Va. Code § 31-1A-1 *et seq.*). The act states generally that an LLC may be formed by any two persons for any lawful purpose and that it may transact "any lawful business that a corporation, general partnership, limited partnership or other business entity may conduct under the laws of [the] state" (W. Va. Code §§ 31-1A-7, 31-1A-3, 31-1A-

4(a)(16)).   Conversations with state regulators revealed differences of opinion about this issue; the secretary of state's office indicated that it considered LLCs unable to practice professions because the professional boards would not permit it, while staff at the professional boards claimed to have no jurisdiction over LLCs and no position on whether they could employ licensees.[169]   In the absence of any limitation on multidisciplinary practice in the medical or psychological practice laws, it could be argued that the LLC is a permissible vehicle for such practice, but this conclusion is not entirely clear.

## D. Networks

West Virginia does not regulate provider networks.   Psychologists, physicians, and allied health professionals may form networks and contract with third-party payers to provide services.


## WISCONSIN

### A. Partnerships

A Wisconsin partnership may be formed to engage in "every trade, occupation, or profession" (Wis. Stat. Ann. § 178.01(2)(b)).   Wayne Austin, counsel to the Office of Board Legal Services (which advises both the medicine and psychology boards), indicated that a joint partnership would be permissible if the state's fee-splitting prohibition was not violated (Wis. Stat. Ann. § 448.08(1)).[170]   On this issue he indicated that the boards relied on a 1982 opinion by the attorney general (71 Op. Atty. Gen. Wis. 108, April 14), wherein the attorney general found no violation of the statute in a physician PC's billing of patients for the services of employee physical therapists.   The fee-splitting law is satisfied, according to the opinion, if the bill identifies the different professionals providing the services and states an "accurate dollar figure" for their respective services.   As long as this billing accuracy is observed, Mr. Austin indicated that the boards consider this opinion to effectively resolve any fee-splitting problems posed by multidisciplinary health practices, including partnerships.   Psychologists, physicians, and allied health professionals may thus practice as partners and employees of a partnership, which may bill for their services.

Wisconsin does not have an LLP law.

### B. *Corporations*

Wisconsin law prohibits the employment of physicians by a business corporation. In a 1986 opinion the state attorney general discussed the issue at length (75 Op. Atty. Gen. Wis 200, October 21) and concluded that the state legislature's adoption of a professional service corporation statute affirmed the common-law corporate practice prohibition. The opinion further concluded that corporate employment of physicians would violate statutes barring the unauthorized practice of medicine and payments by physicians for referrals (Wis. Stat. Ann. §§ 448.03(1), 448.08(1)). It is thus evident that physicians may not practice as employees of Wisconsin business corporations, and Mr. Austin confirmed that this prohibition remains in force.[171] This rule renders a joint physician/psychologist practice, conducted by employees of a business corporation, impermissible.

Corporations owned by professions are known as "service corporations" (SCs) in Wisconsin. An SC's shareholders generally must "all have the same license, certificate or registration," but a 1993 amendment to the law allows different health care professionals to own an SC jointly (Wis. Stat. Ann. § 180.1903(1)). The amendment specifies that licensed physicians and psychologists are health care professionals, so it is clear that they may jointly hold shares, and practice in, an SC (Wis. Stat. Ann. § 180.1901(1)(m)). Mr. Austin confirmed that physicians and psychologists may practice as coowners or employees of an SC under the amendment.[172]

### C. LLCs

The Wisconsin LLC act does not address the provision of professional services by an LLC. The act permits an LLC to be organized "for any lawful purpose," although LLCs are subject to any limitations imposed by any other law regulating the relevant business (Wis. Stat. Ann. § 180.0106(1)). Mr. Austin indicated, however, that the medical and psychological boards do not consider the LLC form to be available for professional services.[173] They consider the reasoning of the 1986 attorney general opinion that upheld the corporate practice of medicine prohibition to apply with equal force to LLCs. The LLC is thus not an option in Wisconsin at present.

## D. Networks

Wisconsin does not have a PPO statute or otherwise limit provider networks. Psychologists, physicians, and allied health professionals may form and contract with networks.


## WYOMING

### A. Partnerships

There do not appear to be any statutory barriers to multidisciplinary partnerships in Wyoming. A partnership may be formed to carry on a business, and "business" is defined to include "every trade, occupation, and profession" (Wyo. Stat. Ann. § 17-21-101(a)(i), Supp. 1994). No section limits partnership practice to a single practice. Psychologists, physicians, and allied health professionals may therefore practice as partners and employees of a partnership. The partnership may bill third-party payers for the professional services of its partners and employees.

Wyoming law does not provide for LLPs, although it is expected that an LLP bill may soon be introduced in the state legislature.


### B. Corporations

The Wyoming business corporation act provides that a business corporation may be formed for any lawful purpose or purposes, provided that a corporation subject to another state statute may incorporate only if permitted by, and subject to all limitations of, the other statute (Wyo. Stat. Ann. § 17-16-301). Other statutes provide that a corporation organized under the general business corporation act, whose capital stock is owned exclusively by licensed professionals, may "practice and offer professional services in such profession" by and through the licensed stockholders or licensed employees (Wyo. Stat. Ann. § 17-3-101). The statute's use of the term "such profession" suggests that such a corporation, the name of which must contain the words "professional corporation" or "PC," is not permitted to offer professional services in more than one discipline (Wyo. Stat. Ann. § 17-3-103). Cathy Reed, a corporate examiner in the secretary of state's corporate division, and Barbara Boyer, the corporation division's attorney in the attorney general's office, confirmed this interpretation.[174]

It could be argued that the PC statute and its single-profession limitation apply only when "all" shareholders of a corporation are professionals. If they are not all professionals, it could be argued that the business corporation act (which contains no single-profession limitation) applies instead and permits corporations to render professional services in more than one discipline. Although Ms. Reed agreed with this interpretation, Ms. Boyer stated that the attorney general's office would likely take the position that a corporation offering professional services may be formed only when it is owned entirely by professionals and only when it complies with the PC statute and its single-profession limitation.[175] Thus, physicians and psychologists would most likely not be permitted to form a corporation under either the PC or business corporation statutes in Wyoming.

## C. LLCs

The Wyoming LLC statute provides that LLCs may be organized for any lawful purpose (other than banking and insurance) and that

> [n]othing in this act shall be interpreted as precluding an individual whose occupation requires licensure from forming a limited liability company if the applicable licensing statutes do not prohibit it and the licensing body does not prohibit it by rule or regulation adopted consistent with the appropriate licensing statute. No limited liability company may offer professional services or practice *a profession* except by and through its licensed members or licensed employees. . . . (Wyo. Stat. Ann. § 17-15-103, Supp. 1994, emphasis added)

Like the PC statute, the LLC statute describes the circumstances under which an LLC may practice a profession, rather than explicitly allowing for practice in multiple professions. Nevertheless, unlike the PC statute, which states that a PC may provide "professional services *in* such profession," the LLC statute states that an LLC may offer "professional services *or* practice a profession." It could be argued, therefore, that an LLC may practice in a single profession or offer professional services in multiple disciplines.

According to Ms. Reed, an LLC may be formed to provide both physician and psychologist services.[176] However, Ms. Boyer said that this issue has not been raised before and suggested that a written request for an opinion be submitted before attempting to form a multidisciplinary LLC.[177]

## D. Networks

Wyoming does not regulate physician networks or have an IPA or PPO statute. Networks of physicians, psychologists, and allied health professionals may contract with third-party payers for the provision of services.

# Notes

[1] A psychologist is personally liable for damages caused by his or her own malpractice, regardless of whether he or she is a sole practitioner or an owner or employee of a partnership, corporation, or limited liability company.

[2] In contrast, a psychologist who is an employee of a partnership may not be held liable for the malpractice of other practitioners who practice through the partnership.

[3] It is not uncommon for even solo practitioners to practice in the form of a PC. Practitioners who are already incorporated and who wish to combine their practices into a larger PC have several options. They can merge their existing PCs into a new PC or they can transfer their practices into a new PC, leaving their original PCs in place to collect accounts receivable. Alternatively, in many states they can establish a structure in which their existing PCs become subsidiaries of a newly created "parent" PC. The choice among these approaches will generally depend on the practitioners' individual financial situations.

[4] In some states (e.g., New York), standard LLCs are prohibited from providing professional services, but specific provisions permit professional LLCs (PLLCs).

[5] The term "independent practice association" (or IPA) is generally applied to a type of network that receives capitated payments from payers. The discussion here applies to IPAs (although IPAs may be subject to particular state regulations). This section also applies to provider-hospital organizations (PHOs), provider organizations (POs), MSOs, and any other organization that does not provide professional services in its own name but instead contracts with independent practitioners.

[6] An alternative approach is that of a "messenger model." In this model each network member is given the opportunity to accept or reject every proposal received by the network. Because this model is cumbersome operationally and because payers are unwilling to negotiate with networks that cannot speak definitively on behalf of their members, networks that have relied on the messenger model have generally been unsuccessful in attracting contracts.

[7] In New York a network may contract with only a single health maintenance organization (HMO), not with any other type of payer.

[8] Telephone Interview with Bill Garrett, Assistant Attorney General who advises Alabama Board of Examiners in Psychology (July 31, 1995).

[9] Telephone Interview with Ken Dowdy, Legal Advisor, Office of the Secretary of State of Alabama (August 3, 1995).

[10] Ibid.

[11] Telephone Interview with Ken Truitt, Assistant Attorney General who advises Alaska

Board of Psychologist and Psychological Associate Examiners and Alaska State Medical Board (July 31, 1995).

[12] Telephone Interview with Mike Monagle, Attorney, Alaska Banking, Securities and Corporations Division (October 25, 1995).

[13] Telephone Interview with Venci Serra, Assistant Attorney General who advises Alaska Banking, Securities and Corporations Division (October 25, 1995).

[14] Telephone Interviews with Mike Monagle, Attorney, Alaska Banking, Securities and Corporations Division (October 25, 1995), and Venci Serra, Assistant Attorney General who advises Alaska Banking, Securities and Corporations Division (October 25, 1995).

[15] Telephone Interview with Nancy Beck, Counsel, Arizona Board of Medical Examiners (February 23, 1995).

[16] Telephone Interview with Cheryl Leon, Examiner, Arizona Corporation Commission (February 24, 1995).

[17] Telephone Interview with Eric Bryant, Assistant Attorney General and Member of Arizona Board of Psychologist Examiners (February 28, 1995).

[18] Effective January 1, 1996, the professional corporation act renumbered, from § 10-901 *et seq.* to § 10-2201 *et seq.*

[19] Telephone Interview with Cheryl Leon, Examiner, Arizona Corporation Commission (February 24, 1995).

[20] The section says that "professional service" is any type of service for which licensure or other authorization is needed; physicians' services are listed as an example, but psychologists' services are not.

[21] Telephone Interview with Ann Purvis, Attorney, Office of the Secretary of State of Arkansas (February 28, 1995).

[22] *Ibid.*

[23] A psychologist may be an employee of an individual physician and, presumably, of a partnership of physicians (see 58 Ops. Atty. Gen. 755, Oct. 3, 1975).

[24] Telephone Interview with Michael Rothman, Director of Policy, Colorado Department of Health Care Policy and Financing (May 2, 1995).

[25] Telephone Interviews with Shannel Lorance, Administrative Officer, Colorado State Board of Medical Examiners (April 27, 1995) and Matthew Norwood, Assistant Attorney General who advises Colorado State Board of Medical Examiners (May 8, 1995).

[26] Telephone Interview with Steve Paull, Secretary, Colorado Board of Psychologist Examiners (May 3, 1995).

[27] Telephone Interview with Matthew Norwood, Assistant Attorney General who advises Colorado State Board of Medical Examiners (May 8, 1995).

[28] *Ibid.*

[29] Telephone Interview with Shannel Lorance, Administrative Officer, Colorado State Board of Medical Examiners (April 27, 1995).

[30] The attorney general concluded, however, that nonprofit hospital corporations were not subject to this restriction.

[31] Telephone Interviews with Joseph Gillen, Director, Licensing Division of Department of Public Health and Addiction Services (February 24, 1995) and Tom Ryan, Attorney, Office of the Secretary of State of Connecticut (February 22, 1995).

[32] Telephone Interview with Juan Reyes, Administrative Officer, Board of Examiners of Psychologists (February 22, 1995).

[33] Telephone Interview with Tom Ryan, Attorney, Office of the Secretary of State of Connecticut (February 22, 1995).

[34] *Ibid.*

[35] *Ibid.*

[36] Telephone Interview with George Coyle, Assistant Secretary of State (April 25, 1995).

[37] Telephone Interview with Malcolm Cobin, Assistant State Solicitor who advises Board of Medical Practice and Board of Examiners of Psychologists (April 25, 1995).

[38] Telephone Interview with George Coyle, Assistant Secretary of State (April 25, 1995).

[39] Telephone Interview with Desiree Jones, Staff, Corporations Division (October 25, 1995).

[40] Letter from James R. Granger, Jr., Acting Executive Director, Board of Medicine, to Thomas J. Walsh (April 5, 1995).

[41] Telephone Interview with Wayne Witkowski, Deputy Corporation Counsel (October 26, 1995).

[42] *Ibid.*

[43] Telephone Interview with Constance Cabral, Executive Officer, Hawaii Board of Medical Examiners (July 31, 1995).

[44] Telephone Interview with James Kobashigawa, Executive Officer, Hawaii Board of Psychology (August 2, 1995).

[45] Telephone Interview with Lauren Namba, Business Regulation Assistant, Hawaii Department of Business Regulation (July 31, 1995).

[46] Telephone Interview with Everett Wohlers, Deputy Secretary of State for Commercial Affairs (July 31, 1995).

[47] Telephone Interview with Nancy Herr, Quality Assurance Specialist, Idaho Board of Medicine (July 31, 1995).

[48] Telephone Interview with Everett Wohlers, Deputy Secretary of State for Commercial Affairs (July 31, 1995).

[49] *Ibid.*

[50] Telephone Interview with Helene Hoffman, General Counsel, Illinois Department of Professional Regulation (May 9, 1995).

[51] *Ibid.*

[52] Telephone Interview with Pat Zander, Staff, Office of the Secretary of State of Illinois (May 8, 1995).

[53] *Ibid.*

[54] *Ibid.*

[55] Telephone Interview with Lisa Perius, Director, Medical Licensing Board of Indiana (March 7, 1995).

[56] Telephone Interview with Nate Feltman, Counsel, Corporations Division, Office of the Secretary of State of Indiana (March 14, 1995).

[57] *Ibid.*

[58] Telephone Interviews with Lisa Perius, Director, Medical Licensing Board of Indiana (March 7, 1995), Barbara McNutt, Director, Indiana State Psychology Board (March 15, 1995), and Nate Feltman, Counsel, Corporations Division, Office of the Secretary of State of Indiana (March 14, 1995).

[59] Telephone Interview with Monte Bratelli, Attorney, Corporations Division, Office of the Secretary of State of Iowa (October 25, 1995).

[60] Telephone Interviews with Julie Pottorff, Deputy Attorney General who advises Iowa

Board of Medical Examiners (October 24, 1995) and Maureen McGuire, Deputy Attorney General who advises Iowa Board of Psychology Examiners (October 24, 1995).

[61] *Ibid.*

[62] Telephone Interview with Monte Bratelli, Attorney, Corporations Division, Office of the Secretary of State of Iowa (October 25, 1995).

[63] Telephone Interviews with Julie Pottorff, Deputy Attorney General who advises Iowa Board of Medical Examiners (October 24, 1995), Maureen McGuire, Deputy Attorney General who advises Iowa Board of Psychology Examiners (October 24, 1995), and Monte Bratelli, Attorney, Corporations Division, Office of the Secretary of State of Iowa (October 25, 1995).

[64] Telephone Interview with Chad Tenpenny, Attorney, Office of the Secretary of State of Indiana (July 17, 1995).

[65] *Ibid.*

[66] Telephone Interview with Wes Faulkner, General Counsel, Kentucky Board of Medical Licensure (March 14, 1995).

[67] Telephone Interviews with Wes Faulkner, General Counsel, Kentucky Board of Medical Licensure (March 14, 1995), and Scott Majors, Assistant Attorney General who advises Kentucky Board of Examiners of Psychologists (March 9, 1995).

[68] Telephone Interviews with Clay Wertz, Attorney, Office of the Secretary of State of Louisiana (October 26, 1995), Robert Conrad, Jr., Attorney who advises Louisiana Board of Medical Examiners (October 30, 1995), and Jim Quillen, M.D., Chairman, Louisiana Board of Examiners of Psychologists (October 25, 1995).

[69] Telephone Interviews with Robert Conrad, Jr., Attorney who advises Louisiana Board of Medical Examiners (October 30, 1995), and Jim Quillen, M.D., Chairman, Louisiana Board of Examiners of Psychologists (October 25, 1995).

[70] Telephone Interview with Clay Wertz, Attorney, Office of the Secretary of State of Louisiana (October 26, 1995).

[71] *Ibid.*

[72] Telephone Interviews with Robert Conrad, Jr., Attorney who advises Louisiana Board of Medical Examiners (October 30, 1995), and Jim Quillen, M.D., Chairman, Louisiana Board of Examiners of Psychologists (October 25, 1995).

[73] Telephone Interview with Steven McKay, Ph.D., Chairman, Maine Board of Examiners of Psychologists (March 14, 1995).

[74] Telephone Interview with Joe Wannamaker, Counsel, Office of the Secretary of State of Maine (March 14, 1995).

[75] Telephone Interview with Joe Stewart, Assistant Attorney General who advises Maryland Department of Assessments and Taxation (May 25, 1995).

[76] Telephone Interview with Carolyn Wescott, Assistant Attorney General who advises Maryland Board of Physician Quality Assurance (May 26, 1995).

[77] *Ibid.*

[78] Telephone Interview with Joe Stewart, Assistant Attorney General who advises Maryland Department of Assessments and Taxation (May 25, 1995).

[79] Telephone Interview with Ray Bailey, Staff Attorney, Office of the Secretary of State of Mississippi (October 24, 1995).

[80] Telephone Interviews with R. Doyle Bradshaw, Executive Officer, Mississippi State Board of Medical Licensure (October 25, 1995), and Stan Ingram, Attorney who advises Mississippi State Board of Medical Licensure (October 25, 1995).

[81] Telephone Interviews with R. Doyle Bradshaw, Executive Officer, Mississippi State Board of Medical Licensure (October 25, 1995), Stan Ingram, Attorney who advises Mississippi State Board of Medical Licensure (October 25, 1995), and Onetta Whitley, Assistant Attorney General who advises Mississippi State Board of Psychological Examiners (October 30, 1995).

[82] Telephone Interviews with Penney Rector, Assistant Attorney General who advises Missouri State Committee of Psychologists (October 30, 1995), and Evan Buchheim, Assistant Attorney General who advises Missouri State Board of Registration for the Healing Arts (October 31, 1995).

[83] Telephone Interviews with Penney Rector, Assistant Attorney General who advises Missouri State Committee of Psychologists (October 30, 1995) and Evan Buchheim, Assistant Attorney General who advises Missouri State Board of Registration for the Healing Arts (October 31, 1995).

[84] *Ibid.*

[85] Telephone Interview with Pat England, Counsel, Montana State Board of Medical Examiners (October 23, 1995).

[86] *Ibid.*

[87] Telephone Interviews with Pat England, Counsel, Montana State Board of Medical Examiners (October 23, 1995), and Cheryl Brandt, Staff, Montana State Board of Psychology (October 24, 1995).

[88] *Ibid.*

[89] Telephone Interview with Greg Lemon, Deputy Secretary of State of Nebraska (October 25, 1995).

[90] Telephone Interviews with Thelma DeYoung, Coordinator, Nebraska Board of Examiners in Medicine and Surgery (October 24, 1995), and Rita Talkin, Staff, Board of Examiners of Psychologists (October 25, 1995).

[91] Telephone Interview with Greg Lemon, Deputy Secretary of State of Nebraska (October 25, 1995).

[92] Telephone Interview with Kateri Cavin, Deputy Attorney General who advises Secretary of State of Nevada (October 24, 1995).

[93] *Ibid.*

[94] Telephone Interviews with Larry Leslie, Counsel, Nevada Board of Medical Examiners (October 24, 1995), and Kateri Cavin, Deputy Attorney General who advises Secretary of State of Nevada (October 24, 1995).

[95] Telephone Interview with Kateri Cavin, Deputy Attorney General who advises Secretary of State of Nevada (October 24, 1995).

[96] *Ibid.*

[97] Telephone Interviews with Larry Leslie, Counsel, Nevada Board of Medical Examiners (October 24, 1995), and Christa Peterson, Ph.D., President, Nevada Board of Psychological Examiners (October 26, 1995).

[98] Telephone Interview with Doug Jones, Assistant Attorney General who advises Nevada Board of Registration in Medicine and Nevada Board of Examiners of Psychology and Mental Health Practice (October 22, 1995).

[99] *Ibid.*

[100] Letter from Deborah T. Poritz, Attorney General of New Jersey, to Mark Herr, Director, New Jersey Division of Consumer Affairs (February 13, 1996).

[101] Telephone Interview with Debra Levine, Deputy Attorney General who advises New Jersey Board of Medical Examiners (May 15, 1996).

[102] Telephone Interviews with G.T.S. Kalca, Counsel, New Mexico Board of Medical Examiners (March 16, 1995), and Gloria Carrillo, Staff, New Mexico Board of Psychologist Examiners (March 15, 1995).

[103] Telephone Interview with Manuel Salinas, Director, Corporations Division, New Mexico Corporation Commission (March 16, 1995).

[104] *Ibid.*

[105] Letter from Kathleen Doyle, Executive Secretary, Board of Psychology, to Sylvan J. Schaffer, New York State Psychological Association, Inc., August 22, 1994.

[106] Letters from John Franzen, Associate Attorney, Office of General Counsel, New York State Department of Health to Matthew D. Babcock (April 18, 1991), and from Joyce Gallimore, Director, Bureau of Alternative Delivery Systems, New York State Department of Health to addressee with name redacted (December 2, 1991).

[107] Telephone Interview with John Collar, Director, Corporations Division, Office of the Secretary of State of North Carolina (May 26, 1995).

[108] Telephone Interview with Jim Wilson, Attorney, North Carolina Board of Medical Examiners (May 26, 1995).

[109] Telephone Interviews with Jim Wilson, Attorney, North Carolina Board of Medical Examiners (May 26, 1995), and Martha Story, Executive Director, North Carolina Board of Practicing Psychologists (May 24, 1995).

[110] Telephone Interviews with Rolf Sletten, Executive Secretary, North Dakota Board of Medical Examiners (October 27, 1995), and Chris Kuchler, Ph.D., President, North Dakota Board of Psychologist Examiners (October 27, 1995).

[111] Telephone Interview with Rolf Sletten, Executive Secretary, North Dakota Board of Medical Examiners (October 27, 1995).

[112] Letter from Nicholas J. Spaeth, North Dakota Attorney General, to Robert G. Hoy, Cass County State's Attorney, October 23, 1990.

[113] Telephone Interview with Vickie Hedges, Enforcement Supervisor, Ohio Board of Psychology (March 24, 1995).

[114] Telephone Interview with Bill Schmidt, Counsel, Ohio Medical Board (March 24, 1995).

[115] Telephone Interview with Katie Phipps, Attorney, Office of the Secretary of State of Ohio (March 24, 1995).

[116] Telephone Interview with Bill Schmidt, Counsel, Ohio Medical Board (March 24, 1995).

[117] Telephone Interview with Katie Phipps, Attorney, Office of the Secretary of State of Ohio (March 24, 1995).

[118] Telephone Interview with Vickie Hedges, Enforcement Supervisor, Ohio Board of Psychology (March 24, 1995).

[119] Moreover, even without enforcement of the corporate practice of medicine doctrine, there is ambiguity about the permissibility of such a multidisciplinary business corporation. The statute's use of the singular term "any profession" suggests that business corporations may only practice one profession. Despite this language, the corporations division of the secretary of state's office, according to Ms. Phipps, takes the position that professionals in multiple disciplines are permitted to form a business corporation together.

[120] Telephone Interview with Katie Phipps, Attorney, Office of the Secretary of State of Ohio (March 24, 1995).

[121] Telephone Interview with Daniel Gamino, Attorney who advises Oklahoma Board of Medical Licensure (August 17, 1995).

[122] Telephone Interview with Joe McCormick, Assistant Attorney General who advises Oklahoma Board of Examiners of Psychologists (August 17, 1995).

[123] Telephone Interview with Daniel Gamino, Attorney who advises Oklahoma Board of Medical Licensure (August 17, 1995), and Joe McCormick, Assistant Attorney General who advises Oklahoma Board of Examiners of Psychologists (August 17, 1995).

[124] *Ibid.*

[125] Telephone Interviews with Lynn Rosik, Assistant Attorney General who advises the Secretary of State of Oregon (August 18, 1995), Paul Sundermier, Assistant Attorney General who advises the Oregon Board of Medical Examiners (August 13, 1995), and Bonnie Wilson, Administrator, Oregon State Board of Psychologist Examiners (August 1, 1995).

[126] Telephone Interview with Paul Sundermier, Assistant Attorney General who advises the Oregon Board of Medical Examiners (August 13, 1995).

[127] Telephone Interview with Bonnie Wilson, Administrator, Oregon State Board of Psychologist Examiners (August 1, 1995).

[128] *Ibid.*

[129] Telephone Interview with Paul Sundermier, Assistant Attorney General who advises the Oregon Board of Medical Examiners (August 13, 1995).

[130] Telephone Interview with April McClaine, Counsel, Pennsylvania State Board of Medicine (June 1, 1995).

[131] *Ibid.*

[132] Letter from April McClaine, Counsel, State Board of Medisine, to Joseph W. Marshall III, January 19, 1995.

[133] Telephone Interview with Lois Fager, Staff, Pennsylvania State Board of Psychology (June 1, 1995).

[134] Telephone Interview with April McClaine, Counsel, Pennsylvania State Board of Medicine (June 1, 1995).

[135] *Ibid.*

[136] Telephone Interview with Bruce McIntyre, Legal Advisor, Rhode Island Board of Medical Licensure and Discipline (August 3, 1995).

[137] Telephone Interview with Vanessa Picard, Staff, Division of Professional Regulation, Rhode Island Department of Health (Auguest 2, 1995).

[138] Telephone Interview with Katherine Merola, Legal Counsel, Office of the Secretary of State of Rhode Island (August 3, 1995).

[139] *Ibid.*

[140] Telephone Interview with Rick Wilson, Counsel, South Carolina Board of Medical Examiners (March 16, 1995).

[141] Telephone Interviews with Rick Wilson, Counsel, South Carolina Board of Medical Examiners (March 16, 1995), and Patti Glenn, Administrator, South Carolina State Board of Examiners in Psychology (March 16, 1995).

[142] Telephone Interview with Rick Wilson, Counsel, South Carolina Board of Medical Examiners (March 16, 1995).

[143] Telephone Interview with Patti Glenn, Administrator, South Carolina State Board of Examiners in Psychology (March 16, 1995).

[144] Telephone Interview with Sherry Sundem-Wald, Deputy Attorney General who advises the Office of the Secretary of State of South Dakota (October 30, 1995).

[145] Telephone Interviews with Sharvin Dixon, Director, South Dakota Board of Medical and Osteopathic Examiners (October 25, 1995), and Carol Tellinghuysen, Director, South Dakota Board of Psychology (October 25, 1995).

[146] *Ibid.*

[147] *Ibid.*

[148] Telephone Interview with Bob Kramer, Associate General Counsel, Tennessee Department of Health (July 26, 1995).

[149] *Ibid.*

[150] Telephone Interview with Bill Young, Deputy Commissioner, Tennessee Department of Commerce and Insurance (July 31, 1995).

[151] Telephone Interview with Ray Walker, Counsel, Division of Professional Licensing, Utah Department of Commerce (May 25, 1995).

[152] Telephone Interview with George Daniels, Counsel, Division of Corporations and Commercial Code, Utah Department of Commerce (June 2, 1995).

[153] Telephone Interview with Ray Walker, Counsel, Division of Professional Licensing, Utah Department of Commerce (May 25, 1995).

[154] Telephone Interview with George Daniels, Counsel, Division of Corporations and Commercial Code, Utah Department of Commerce (June 2, 1995).

[155] *Ibid.*

[156] Telephone Interviews with Sienna Walton, Counsel, Vermont Board of Medical Practice (May 25, 1995), and John Chase, Attorney who advises Vermont Board of Psychological Examiners, Office of the Secretary of State of Vermont (May 26, 1995).

[157] Telephone Interview with John Chase, Attorney, Office of the Secretary of State of Vermont (May 26, 1995).

[158] *Ibid.*

[159] Telephone Interview with Sandra Thompson, Staff, Virginia Corporation Commission (April 24, 1995).

[160] Telephone Interview with Lynn Fleming, Assistant Attorney General who advises the Virginia Board of Medicine (April 24, 1995).

[161] *Ibid.*

[162] Telephone Interview with Emerson Wilbey, Legal Advisor, Virginia Corporation Commission (April 24, 1995).

[163] *Ibid.*

[164] *Ibid.*

[165] *Ibid.*

[166] Telephone Interview with Linda Bond, Attorney, Corporations Division, Office of the Secretary of State of Washington (December 4, 1994).

[167] Telephone Interview with Deborah Lewis Rodecker, Legal Counsel, Board of Medicine (August 18, 1995).

[168] *Ibid.*

[169] Telephone Interviews with Steven Reed, Attorney, Office of the Secretary of State of West Virginia (August 17, 1995), Doug Douglas, Administrator, West Virginia Board of Examiners of Psychologists (July 31, 1995), and Deborah Lewis Rodecker, Legal Counsel, Board of Medicine (August 18, 1995).

[170] Telephone Interview with Wayne Austin, Counsel, Office of Board Legal Services (July 20, 1995).

[171] *Ibid.*

[172] *Ibid.*

[173] *Ibid.*

[174] Telephone Interviews with Cathy Reed, Corporate Examiner, Corporations Division, Office of the Secretary of State of Wyoming (March 23, 1995), and Barbara Boyer, Assistant Attorney General who advises the Corporations Division, Office of the Secretary of State of Wyoming (March 23, 1995).

[175] *Ibid.*

[176] Telephone Interview with Cathy Reed, Corporate Examiner, Corporations Division, Office of the Secretary of State of Wyoming (March 23, 1995).

[177] Telephone Interview with Barbara Boyer, Assistant Attorney General who advises the Corporations Division, Office of the Secretary of State of Wyoming (March 23, 1995).

# Glossary

Access  Patients' ability to obtain needed health services. Measures of access include the location of health facilities and their hours of operation, patient travel time and distance to health facilities, the availability of medical services, and the cost of care.

Capitation  Method of payment for health care services in which the provider accepts a fixed amount of payment per subscriber, per period of time, in return for specified services over a specified period of time.

Carrier  Any commercial insurance company.

Carve Out  An arrangement in which coverage for a specific category of services (e.g., mental health/substance abuse, vision care, prescription drugs) is provided through a contract with a separate set of providers. The contract may specify certain payment and utilization management arrangements.

Case Management  Monitoring, planning, and coordination of treatment rendered to patients with conditions that are expected to require high cost or extensive services. Case management is focused and longitudinal, usually following the patient for 3 to 6 months minimum to avoid hsopital readmission.

Central Processing Unit (CPU)  The computer's brain, which largely determines the speed and cost of hardware.

Claims Review  A review of claims by government, medical foundations, professional review organizations, insurers, or others responsible for payment to determine liability and amount of payment.

Concurrent Review  Third party review of the medical necessity, level of care, length of stay, appropriateness of services, and discharge plan for a patient in a health care facility. Occurs at the time the patient is treated.

Continuum of Care  In behavioral health, generally defined as the spectrum of care delivered in residential treatment, inpatient, partial hospitalization, home health, and outpatient settings.

COPAYMENT   Type of cost sharing whereby insured or covered person pays a specified flat fee per unit of service or unit of time (e.g., $10 per office visit, $25 per inpatient hospital day); insurance covers the remainder of the cost.

COST CONTAINMENT   Actions taken by employers and insurers to curtail health care costs (e.g., increasing employee cost sharing, requiring second opinions, preadmission screening).

COST SHARING   Requirement that health care consumers contribute to their own medical care costs through deductibles and coinsurance or copayments.

CREDENTIALING   Process of reviewing a practitioner's credentials (i.e., training, experience, demonstrated ability) for the purpose of determining whether criteria for clinical privileges have been met.

DIAGNOSTIC RELATED GROUPS (DRGs)   Reimbursement methodology whereby hospitals receive a fixed fee per patient based on the admitting diagnosis regardless of the length of stay or amount of services received.

ENROLLMENT   Means by which a person establishes membership in a group insurance plan.

EXCESS CHARGES   Portion of any charge greater than the usual and prevailing charge for a service. A charge is "usual and prevailing" when it does not exceed the typical charge of the provider in the absence of insurance and when it is no greater than the general level of charges for comparable services and supplies made by other providers in the same area.

FEE FOR SERVICE   In the traditional fee-for-service model, the provider bills the patient or payer for a specified amount, typically on the basis of the amount of time spent delivering the service. Until recently, providers determined the fees charged for services and customary fees were generally accepted. Now, providers may be required to accept a payer's fee schedule, which demands that a certain fee be accepted as payment in full. PPOs represent an attempt to save the fee-for-service method of payment by regulating the cost of treatment in the context of a traditional reimbursement plan.

FEE SCHEDULE   A listing of accepted fees or predetermined monetary allowances for specified services and procedures.

FREE-STANDING FACILITY   Health care center that is physically separated from a hospital or other institution of which it is a legal part or with which it is affiliated, or an independently operated or owned private or public business or enterprise providing limited health care services or a range of services, such as ambulatory surgery, hemodialysis treatment, diagnostic tests, or examinations.

GATEKEEPING   Process by which a primary care provider directly provides primary care to patients and coordinates all diagnostic testing and specialty referrals required for patients' medical care. Referrals must be preauthorized by the gatekeeper unless there is an emergency. Gatekeeping is a subset of the functions of a primary provider's case manager.

GROUP CONTRACT   Arrangement between a managed care company and the subscribing group that contains rates, performance covenants, relationships among parties, schedule of benefits, and other conditions. The term is generally limited to a 12-month period but may be renewed.

GROUP PRACTICE   A group of practitioners organized as a private partnership, limited liability company, or corporation; participating practitioners share facilities and personnel as well as the earnings from their practice. The providers who make up a practice may represent either a single specialty or a range of specialties.

HEALTH MAINTENANCE ORGANIZATION (HMO)   Health care delivery system that provides comprehensive health services to an enrolled population frequently for a prepaid fixed (capitated) payment, although other payment arrangements can be made. The organization consists of a network of health care providers rendering a wide range of health services and assumes the financial risks of providing these services. Enrollees generally are not reimbursed for care provided outside the HMO network.

INDEMNITY INSURANCE PLAN   An insurance plan that pays specific dollar amounts to an insured individual for specific services and procedures without guaranteeing complete coverage for the full cost of health care services.

INDIVIDUAL PRACTICE ASSOCIATION (IPA) MODEL HMO   An organization that contracts with individual health care professionals to provide services in their own offices for enrollees of a health plan. Specialists are generally paid on a fee-for-service basis, but primary care providers may receive capitated payments.

INTEGRATED CARE    Alternative health care delivery system developed by the American Psychological Association in response to the rising cost of providing health care services. It is based on six concepts: Benefit Design, Case Management and Utilization Review, Communications, Direct Contracting, Network Development, and Outcomes.

INTEGRATED DELIVERY SYSTEM (IDS)    System of behavioral health care that offers "one-stop shopping" to potential payers, meaning that a payer can write one check for the entire delivery of care without having to independently negotiate terms with multiple unconnected providers. IDSs offer a full continuum of care, so patients and premiums are managed within one accountable plan's network of providers.

LEVERAGE    A managed care strategy for controlling costs by steering patients to lower-cost providers called substitutes. In behavioral health care, a clinical social worker's psychiatric nurse may be a substitute for a psychologist.

MANAGED CARE    A means of providing health care services in a defined network of health care providers who are given the responsibility to manage and provide quality, cost-effective care. Increasingly, the term is being used by many analysts to include (in addition to HMOs) PPOs and even forms of indemnity insurance coverage that incorporate preadmission certification and other utilization controls.

MENTAL HEALTH AND DRUG ABUSE SERVICES    There are three basic types of mental health services: inpatient care provided in short term psychiatric units in a general hospital or specialized psychiatric facility; outpatient care for individual or group counseling; and partial hospitalization, a combination of both of the above. See also Employee Assistance Program.

MONITOR    The video display portion of a computer system.

MSO    An entity that usually contracts with practitioner groups, independent practice associations, and medical foundations to provide a range of services required in medical practices, such as accounting, utilization review, and staffing.

MULTISPECIALTY GROUP    Group of doctors who represent various specialties and work together in a group practice.

NETWORK    Group of providers who mutually contract with carriers or employers to provide health care services to participants in a specified managed care plan. A contract determines the payment method and rates, utilization controls, and target utilization rates by plan participants.

NETWORKING   To conect computer systems electronically so that users may share files or printers.

PEER REVIEW   Evaluation by practicing providers (or other qualified professionals) of the quality and efficiency of services ordered or performed by other practicing providers. Medical practices, inpatient hospital and extended care facility analyses, utilization reviews, medical audits, ambulatory care, and claims reviews are all aspects of peer review.

PER DIEM   Negotiated daily rate for delivery of all inpatient hospital services provided in one day regardless of the actual services provided. Per diems can also be developed by the type of care provided (e.g., one per diem rate for adult mental health, a different rate for adolescent substance abuse treatment).

PERFORMANCE STANDARDS   Standards that an individual provider is expected to meet, especially with respect to quality of care. The standards may define the volume of care delivered in a specified time period.

PERIPHERALS Optional hardware devices that can be connected to a computer system via cables (e.g., a printer).

POOL   A large number of small groups or individuals who are analyzed and rated as a single large group for insurance purposes. A risk pool may be any account that attempts to find the claims liability for a group with a common denominator.

PREADMISSION REVIEW   When a provider requests that a patient be hospitalized, another opinion may be sought by the insurer. The second provider reviews the treatment plan, evaluates the patient's condition, and confirms the request for admission or recommends another course of action. Similar to second opinions on surgery.

PREAUTHORIZATION   Review and approval of covered benefits, based on a provider's treatment plan. Some insurers require preauthorization for certain high-cost procedures. Others apply the preauthorization requirement when charges exceed a specified dollar amount.

PRECERTIFICATION   Review of the necessity and length of a recommended hospital stay. Often, certification prior to admission is required for nonemergencies and within 48 hours of admission for emergency treatment.

PREFERRED PROVIDER ORGANIZATION   (PPO) Selective contracting agreement with a specified network of health care providers at reduced or negotiated payment rates. In exchange for reduced rates, providers frequently receive expedited claims payments and/or a reasonably predictable market share of patients. Employees may have financial incentives to utilize PPO providers.

PROVIDER   Health care professional (or facility) licensed to provide one or more health care services to patients.

PROVIDER-HOSPITAL ORGANIZATION   Vertically integrated delivery system formed by practitioners and a hospital.

QUALITY ASSURANCE   Activities and programs intended to ensure the quality of care in a defined medical setting or program. Such programs include methods for documenting clinical practice, educational components intended to remedy identified deficiencies in quality, as well as the components necessary to identify and correct such deficiencies (such as peer or utilization review), and a formal process to assess a program's own effectiveness.

QUALITY MANAGEMENT   A participative intervention in which employees and managers continuously review the quality of the services they provide. The process identifies problems, tests solutions to those problems, and constantly monitors solutions for improvement.

REQUEST FOR PROPOSAL (RFP)   Formal document soliciting bids from system vendors.

RISK   The chance or possibility of loss. Risk sharing is often employed as a utilization control mechanism in HMOs. Risk is often defined in insurance terms as the possibility of loss associated with a given population.

SELECTIVE CONTRACTING   Negotiation by third-party payers of a limited number of contracts with health care professionals and facilities in a given service area. Preferential reimbursement practices and/or benefits are then offered to patients seeking care from these providers.

SOFTWARE   Computer programs used to instruct computer hardware on how to perform.

STAFF MODEL HMO   An HMO in which professional providers in a multispecialty group are salaried employees of the HMO.

SUBSTITUTE   A provider who replaces another despite differences in training and licensing scope. A clinical social worker and a psychiatric nurse may be substitutes for each other.

SUPPORT   Assistance provided by a computer vendor after a sale, including training, maintenance, and trouble-shooting.

THIRD PARTY ADMINISTRATOR   Outside company responsible for handling claims and performing administrative tasks associated with health insurance plan maintenance.

THIRD-PARTY PAYER   An organization that pays or insures health care expenses on behalf of beneficiaries or recipients who pay premiums for such coverage.

USUAL, CUSTOMARY, AND REASONABLE (UCR)   Charges considered reasonable and that do not exceed those customarily charged for the same service by other providers in the area.

UTILIZATION REVIEW   Independent determination of whether health care services are appropriate and medically necessary on a prospective, concurrent, and/or retrospective basis to ensure that appropriate and necessary services are provided. Frequently used to curtail the provision of inappropriate services and/or to ensure that services are provided in the most cost-effective manner.

VALUE-BASED PURCHASING   Selection of a product or service based on criteria other than unit price. Value criteria may include quality, outcome, and access.